# KLOPP

*Dare To Dream*

## Andrew Waller

PITCHSIDE
PUBLISHING

# CONTENTS

# PREFACE: KLOPP'S JOURNEY - FROM GLATTEN TO GLORY

"I am not a dreamer. I am a football romantic." - Jurgen Klopp

In the heart of Liverpool, where the River Mersey winds its way through the city, there's a legendary tale etched into the very soul of football. It's a story filled with dreams, determination, and the kind of passion that sends shivers down your spine. At the centre of it all is a man whose name rings out with triumph and love - Jürgen Klopp.

This biography is your ticket to a journey through the life and times of a man who's more than just a football manager; he's a phenomenon. Our story kicks off in the quiet town of Glatten, Germany, where a young Klopp first caught the football bug. Little did anyone know that this spirited young man would rise to become one of the biggest icons in the history of the beautiful game.

As you flip through the chapters ahead, you'll witness the meteoric ascent of a football genius, a guy whose tactical brilliance and magnetic personality would set clubs on fire. But this isn't just about formations and strategies; it's about the man beneath the tactics, the soul behind the genius.

You'll step onto the pitch alongside Klopp as he steers Borussia Dortmund to Bundesliga glory, crafting a team that captured the world's imagination. You'll feel the electric vibes of Anfield as Klopp takes the reins at Liverpool FC, sparking a revival that ended 30 years of hurt.

But this biography isn't just about the wins and trophies. It takes you deep into the personal moments that define Klopp - his early days, his battles, funny stories, and the turning points that forged his character. You'll dive into the nuances of his leadership style, the relentless pursuit of excellence, and the unwavering loyalty he commands from his players.

Within these pages, you'll experience the highs and lows, the heartaches and the exultations, and those unforgettable European nights at Anfield where Klopp's magic unfolded. You'll get a glimpse of the challenges faced during the pandemic-hit season, where lifting the Premier League trophy in an empty stadium became a symbol of resilience.

This is a journey through the life of a man who hasn't just won titles, but has won over hearts. It's a tale of 'heavy metal' football, epic comebacks, and the deafening roar of the Kop. It's a celebration of the champions of England and the everlasting legacy of Jürgen Klopp.

So, football fans, strap in for an incredible ride! We're taking you from the cobblestone streets of Germany to the sacred turf of Anfield. Prepare to be immersed in the world of Jürgen Klopp, where the love for football knows no limits, and the quest for glory is relentless. This is the story of a football maestro, and trust us, you won't want to miss a single page.

# ABOUT THE AUTHOR

Andrew Waller, a renowned online writer and fervent Liverpool fan boasts an impressive portfolio in online journalism. Born and raised in Merseyside, William's childhood was steeped in the local football culture, with his family's loyalties divided between Liverpool and Everton - his mam was a Red and his dad a Blue. He chose the Red path! He fondly recalls the era of Kenny Dalglish and Graeme Souness, whose performances when he visited Anfield left a lasting impact on him.

His career as a writer took off with a focus on sports journalism in Uni, where he distinguished himself with insightful analyses and in-depth coverage of football. Over the years, Andrew has contributed to numerous sports websites, blogs, and magazines, earning recognition for his engaging and informed style.

A highlight of his career has been his extensive coverage of Jürgen Klopp's journey as a manager. Andrew has followed Klopp's career right from its early days in Germany, through to his transformative tenure at Liverpool. His admiration for Klopp's management style and philosophy is evident in his writings, where he often praises Klopp's ability to blend tactical acumen with motivational skills.

For Andrew writing this book is not just a professional milestone but also a personal honour, representing his journey from a young fan watching games at Anfield to a respected writer chronicling the tales of his beloved team and its iconic manager.

# PART I: THE MAKING OF A MAESTRO

# CHAPTER 1: EARLY YEARS IN GLATTEN

In the peaceful town of Glatten, nestled in the beautiful Black Forest of Germany, something significant happened in June 1967. Jürgen Klopp was born, a name that would later become famous in football all around the world. Jürgen wasn't just any addition to the Klopp family; he was the son that his dad, Norbert, had been eagerly waiting for. Before Jürgen came along, his mum, Elisabeth, had two daughters, so his arrival was a big deal for the family.

His parents, Norbert and Elisabeth, taught him important values like working hard, never giving up, and having faith, which would become a big part of who he was.

## His Father's Influence

Jürgen's ascent to football management greatness

is deeply rooted in the early influence of his father, Norbert Klopp. Norbert's role extended beyond the paternal to that of a mentor and coach, ingraining in young Jürgen the principles of hard work, resilience, and a relentless pursuit of excellence.

Norbert Klopp, a fervent sports enthusiast himself, was keen on instilling in Jürgen a strong foundation in football. He initiated training routines with young Jürgen that were not only physically demanding but also mentally challenging. Jürgen's early experiences under his father's tutelage were a blend of rigorous physical training and tactical understanding of the game. Norbert's approach was encapsulated in Jürgen's own words: "My dad was a natural coach, a tough one. He'd say, 'Go!' and I'd ask, 'Why are we doing this?' We kept doing it until I finally beat him, which took about six years. I was really fast, and he made me even quicker." These sessions were critical in shaping Jürgen's physical attributes and understanding of the game.

Instilling Discipline and Resilience

Norbert's coaching style was characterised by a strict discipline and a no-nonsense approach. He believed in the power of hard work and resilience, values that he diligently worked to instil in Jürgen. The daily races and football drills were more than just physical exercises; they were lessons in perseverance and mental toughness. Norbert pushed Jürgen to the limits, fostering a mindset of continuous improvement and never settling for mediocrity.

The influence of Norbert extended beyond the realms of football. He was instrumental in teaching Jürgen life lessons that would later become integral to his personality and coaching style. He emphasised the importance of hard work, resilience, and the relentless pursuit of one's goals. These lessons transcended the football field, shaping Jürgen's approach to life and his interactions with people.

The lessons Jürgen learned from his father significantly influenced his coaching philosophy. Norbert's balanced approach of discipline mixed with empathy is mirrored in Jürgen's managerial style. Jürgen's ability to connect with his players on a personal level while maintaining high standards of performance is a direct reflection of the values instilled in him by his father. The emotional intelligence and tactical acumen that Jürgen exhibits can be traced back to the foundational lessons from Norbert.

Norbert's Enduring Legacy

Norbert's impact on Jürgen's life and career cannot be overstated. His teachings and principles have been a guiding force in Jürgen's journey. The discipline, work ethic, and resilience that Norbert ingrained in Jürgen have become synonymous with his coaching identity. Norbert's legacy lives on through Jürgen, not only in his professional achievements but also in his approach to leadership and life.

## Swabian Roots

"Swabian people take a little while to warm up, but once you are friends, you are friends for life," Jens Haas reflected, painting a picture of the environment that honed Klopp's loyalty and dedication. This same dedication that Jurgen would eventually pour into every team he coached.

But it wasn't just the Swabian culture that nurtured Klopp's growth; it was the people—his sisters, who provided the care and support a young boy needed, and of course, his father. Ulrich Rath, Klopp's first coach and the founder of the local Under-11s, saw that spark early on.

"His father brought the carnival spirit from Rhineland-Palatinate, and Jurgen inherited that fervour, that ability to ignite enthusiasm," recalled Rath. Even at a young age, Klopp wasn't just participating; he was orchestrating, leading, and rallying his teammates with a booming "Let's go!"

## Youth Teams and Early Football Experience

Klopp's first foray into organised football was with

SV Glatten, a local club that provided the platform for his early development. The club, deeply rooted in the community, played a significant role in nurturing his talent. There, Klopp's natural affinity for the game was evident. Jens Haas, a childhood friend and fellow player at SV Glatten, recalls the days when football was a daily ritual: "Back in the early 1970s 'either we were kicking the ball about or training'. Football every day. Homework? 'If at all possible none at all.'"

At SV Glatten, Klopp's leadership qualities and football skills were already noticeable. Haas reminisced about how Klopp was always the first pick during their kickabouts, a testament to his early prowess in the sport: "Klopp was a first pick and he wasn't." This preference by his peers highlighted Klopp's standout abilities even at a young age.

Education and Schooling

Klopp's education played a parallel and significant role in his development. He attended primary school in Glatten, where, alongside his peers, he navigated the challenges and joys of early education. A photograph from his school days shows a young Klopp among twenty-three other children, more girls than boys, a snapshot of his early life in the educational system.

During his time at school, Klopp balanced his love for football with his academic responsibilities.

Even then, his personality traits that would later define his coaching style were budding. His schooling was not just about academics; it was about developing life skills, building relationships, and understanding the value of teamwork and community.

Transition to Advanced Teams

As Klopp grew older, his football journey took him beyond the confines of SV Glatten. His talents were recognized, and he made a significant move to TuS Ergenzingen, a club in a small town fifteen miles east of Glatten. This club had a reputation for nurturing young talent, and it was here that Klopp continued to hone his skills.

This transition was not just about changing clubs; it also coincided with a change in schools. Klopp was one of three from Glatten to attend the grammar school in Dornstetten. This period marked a critical phase in his development, both as a student and a footballer. The move to a new school and club signified a stepping stone towards greater challenges and opportunities.

Throughout these early years, Klopp's character was as much a part of his development as his football skills. His ability to inspire, lead, and bring out the best in those around him was evident from these formative years. Haas noted, "Klopp 'radiated composure'...He was a 'central figure' who you could rely on 'in any situation on the pitch.'" These attributes would become hallmarks of his managerial style in the future.

Klopp's journey through his youth teams and schooling laid the groundwork for his future successes. His experiences during this time were crucial in shaping his approach to football and life. They instilled in him a deep understanding of the game, a robust work ethic, and the ability to connect with and motivate people, qualities that he would carry with him throughout his career.

# CHAPTER 2: MAINZ'S WARRIOR

Klopp spent most of his playing career at Mainz 05. He joined the club's youth academy in 1980, and made his senior debut in 1987. He went on to play over 300 games, scoring 52 goals. He was initially deployed as a striker, but was later moved to defence.

Klopp was known for his work ethic, passion, and leadership, as well as his sense of humour and his ability to connect with his teammates. Hismost notable achievement as a player was helping Mainz to win the 2. Bundesliga in 2003–04. He was also a key member of the team that reached the semi-finals of the DFB-Pokal in 2000–01.

## The Darkest Hour

In February 2001, the mood at FSV Mainz 05 was gloomy. Just the day before, they faced their arch-rivals, SpVGG Greuther Fürth, at the Playmobil-

Stadion. It turned out to be a match they'd rather forget. The final score was 3-1 in favour of Fürth, but the pain went beyond just losing the game.

Klopp, their star player, had been dealing with an injury, and ironically, he had one of his worst performances. He got substituted out twenty minutes before full time. This defeat pushed Mainz 05 deeper into the dreaded relegation zone. To say they were in trouble is an understatement. They were in a real mess, stuck at the very bottom of the table with no sign of hope in sight. The number of people coming to watch their games was as low as 3,000, and it felt like nobody cared about their fate anymore.

A Carnival in Full Swing

Interestingly, while Mainz was going through this dark period, the rest of the city was having a blast. It was Rose Monday, a day famous for carnival celebrations in Rhineland-Palatinate's capital. Mainz transformed into a lively and colourful place as half a million folks dressed up in crazy costumes, had some fun, and let loose. The streets were filled with energy, laughter, and maybe a bit too much partying. State broadcasters ARD and ZDF even dedicated a whole evening to the wild gatherings of the city's carnival clubs at the Electoral Palace, where people cracked jokes and made fun of politics, all while enjoying some beer.

A Coach's Dilemma

As the city enjoyed the carnival's happy vibe, the Mainz 05 team faced a big problem. Their coach, Eckhart Krautzun, known as 'Weltenbummler' or the globetrotter because of his extensive coaching career, was worried that the carnival might distract the team from their upcoming crucial match against Duisburg on Ash Wednesday. Things were looking grim, especially after their tough loss in Fürth.

Jürgen Kramny, who was roommates with Jürgen Klopp at the time, remembered, "After losing in Fürth, things were really bad in Mainz. We knew they might either fire the coach or give us a good kick to get us going. We were stuck in a hotel in Bad Kreuznach for three days, so nobody could go out and party." Keeping the players away from the carnival was a clear sign of how serious their situation was.

## A Tough Situation

Christian Heidel, the guy in charge of Mainz 05, decided not to join the carnival festivities either. The team's tough situation was weighing heavily on his mind, leaving no room for fun and games. It was clear that something had to change, and getting rid of the coach seemed like the only way forward. Eckhart Krautzun, despite being a likeable figure with a colourful coaching history that included coaching none other than Diego Maradona, hadn't been able to turn things around since he took over in November. Their terrible record of just six points from nine games was a clear sign that they were heading for relegation.

Heidel couldn't help but feel like Krautzun had tricked him into hiring him as the coach in the first place. Mainz 05 was in a tight spot, and it was time for a new direction, a change that would end up reshaping the club's future.

# CHAPTER 3: FROM PLAYER TO COACH

In the wild world of football, where every match is a rollercoaster ride of emotions, there are moments that just defy all expectations. Mainz found themselves in a really tough spot. They were on the brink of getting relegated. Mainz was stuck in the second division of German football, and their future looked uncertain. It was a critical situation.

## A Bold Move

At the heart of Mainz's quest to turn things around was Christian Heidel, the club's general manager. Heidel's love for Mainz ran deep, and he felt the weight of the club's problems on his shoulders. He knew that they needed a new coach if they were going to save their season. Heidel was a determined guy, and he set out on a mission to find the right coach who could rescue Mainz from their dire situation.

Heidel made a gutsy decision that changed Mainz's history. With the club's survival hanging by a thread, he took a bold step and appointed Klopp as the manager. It was a choice driven by instinct and desperation, something that went against the usual way of doing things. You see, Klopp wasn't some experienced manager; he was a player, a fiery leader on the field. But Heidel saw something special in Klopp, something that was beyond the ordinary.

## Early Management Missteps

When Klopp took the reins, he was diving headfirst into waters he'd never swum in before. He was switching from being one of the lads to the one making the tough calls – transforming from Mainz's reliable player into their gaffer. And he had to do it overnight with friends who had only known him as "Kloppo," the guy they'd battled alongside on the pitch.

The first real test of his newfound authority was picking the starting lineup. Klopp, with his heart set on being upfront and personal, decided he'd deliver the news face-to-face. So there he was, knocking on hotel doors, sitting players down in their rooms, one by one, to deliver their fate.

"Well, this was a very bad plan, because we had twin hotel rooms. So you can imagine it. I get to the first room, and I sit the two players down on the bed, and I turn to one and say, 'You are starting tomorrow.'" Followed by the less enviable, "Unfortunately, you are not starting tomorrow." That's when he was hit with the big, puppy-dog eyes and the innocent, "But... Kloppo... why?"

In that moment, it dawned on him – his approach might have been a bit naive. You can't start everyone, but try explaining that to a room full of your former teammates who still think of you as part of the squad.

Klopp's tale goes on, room after room, the same awkward scene playing out. Eight more times he had to repeat the act, each "You're not starting" echoing louder than the last. By his own admission, it was agonising!

He puts it quite simply, "This was the first of many, many, times that I stepped in the s*** as a manager." His solution? Grab a tissue, clean it off, and learn. Because that's what you do in football – and in life. You make mistakes, you face them, and you grow. And if there's one thing Klopp's become known for, it's turning those lessons into success.

## Staying Up

Under his leadership, the team secured their spot in the league, which was nothing short of incredible considering where they were just a short while beforehand. This quick turnaround showed Klopp's amazing ability to inspire and lead, even when the odds were stacked against him.

Klopp's way of playing became the foundation of Mainz's success. He took over Wolfgang Frank's aggressive and pressing football philosophy and turned it into something formidable. With Klopp in charge, Mainz rediscovered their style of play in the 4-4-2 formation, a system they once thrived in.

"The key to his success was his tactical plan," Christian Heidel stressed. Klopp's careful planning and smart strategies breathed new life into the team. He had a vision, and he executed it brilliantly.

Klopp's influences came from all over the place, drawing from his experiences and the people who had shaped him. His father, Norbert, had been a promising goalkeeper in his youth, and he taught Klopp the values of hard work and discipline. It was a father-son bond built on football, where they faced challenges together and celebrated victories together. Norbert's influence on Klopp's character and work ethic would stay with him throughout his career.

Wolfgang Frank's methods had been successful but were tough for other coaches to replicate. Klopp absorbed what Frank taught him and turned it into a powerful tool for Mainz's comeback. Frank's legacy became a part of Klopp's coaching style.

## The Making of a Manager

Klopp's personal history played a big role in shaping his resilience and how he saw pressure and disappointment. He started his professional football career later than most, and he faced the challenge of breaking into the top leagues. These early struggles gave him a determination and a unique perspective on the pressures that football can bring.

"That was real pressure," Klopp remembered. "We only knew we'd get paid for the next 12 months once the team was safe from relegation." It was a stark reminder of the financial uncertainties that hung over football, even at the highest levels. Klopp's experiences as a player dealing with these uncertainties would shape his outlook as a coach.

A Special Connection with Fans

Klopp's charisma and leadership weren't just confined to the training ground; they also shone when he interacted with fans. He had this amazing ability to connect with supporters on a personal level, to make them believe in the team's mission.

Even after missing out on promotion, Klopp lifted Mainz fans' spirits with his unwavering optimism and deep passion for the club. His words struck a chord with the faithful fans and left a lasting impact on the city. "We'll be back, no question!"

This connection with the supporters wasn't just a one-time thing; it would become a defining feature of Klopp's career as a manager. His knack for uniting fans and players under a common banner of passion and commitment would serve him well in the years ahead.

Klopp's journey in football was a testament to his never-give-up attitude. His late start in professional football and his early struggles had toughened him up and shaped his career. Klopp knew the value of hard work and persistence, and those qualities would define his career as a manager.

Consistency in Being Himself

All through his career, Klopp stayed true to himself and his principles. He earned the respect and admiration of everyone around him. Christian Heidel, who had known Klopp for three decades, vouched for his unwavering authenticity.

"I've known Jürgen for 30 years now, and he's always been the same. He's authentic," Heidel emphasised.

# CHAPTER 4: THE MAINZ ASCENDANCY

In his first full season as the boss in 2001–02, Klopp wasted no time in putting his tactical magic to work. He loved pressing and counter-pressing, and he brought a new sense of energy to the team.

Mainz's performance in that season was really impressive. They finished 4th in the league, just barely missing out on promotion. It was a great start to Klopp's career as a manager, and it gave us a taste of what was coming next.

## Narrow Misses and Never Giving Up

The next season, 2002–03, Mainz ended up in 4th place again, and this time they missed promotion by the tiniest of margins—goal difference. These close calls were frustrating, no doubt, but they also showed how Klopp could push the team right to the edge of success.

But even when things didn't go their way, Klopp never lost his determination. In the 2003–04 season, Mainz finally did it! They finished third and got promoted to the Bundesliga, which is the top German football league. It was a huge moment that proved Klopp was a tactical genius and a great leader.

## Defying the Odds

Mainz's first season in the Bundesliga in 2004–05 was met with doubt. They had the smallest budget and the smallest stadium in the league, and everyone thought they'd struggle. But Klopp had other plans.

They finished 11th, which was pretty darn good for a newcomer. It showed that Klopp could make the most out of his squad. In the next season, 2005–06, they finished 11th again and even qualified for the UEFA Cup in 2005–06. That's a big deal in European football, and it was all thanks to Klopp's tactics.

Sure, they got knocked out early by the eventual champions Sevilla in the UEFA Cup, but Mainz had made their mark in Europe.

## The Santa Claus Story

Klopp recounts a story from his days at Mainz, "We had a Christmas break and friends of ours wanted to have a party in the city." It was during a challenging time for the club, languishing at the bottom of the Bundesliga table. "Nobody had seen me because I had a mask," Klopp said.

His disguise was none other than Santa Claus himself. But the fun led to a slip. "When you are a little bit drunk, so I lifted the mask and then the next thing there is a picture," Klopp revealed.

The next day 'Bild' reported, 'That is how Klopp celebrates 18th place'. It is not actually like I celebrated but it was the picture."

The 2006–07 season was tough for Mainz. They got relegated from the Bundesliga, which was a major setback. But Klopp stayed loyal to the club and decided to stick around.

## 2007/08 Season: Trial by Fire

In the wake of a gut-wrenching relegation, Klopp led Mainz into the seclusion of Thuringia's forests. It was here, in 2007, that Klopp sought to shape a new path for his squad—away from the trappings of modern football and back to basics.

Neven Subotić, one of the youthful prospects in Klopp's care, recalls the tough mornings: the wake-up calls of either Nana Mouskouri or Ireen Sheer's 'Guten Morgen, Sonnenschein', ringing out as a rallying cry for the day ahead. "We were totally shot every morning," Subotić recalls, yet the routine stood as a testament to Klopp's unorthodox methods—peeling carrots and stirring soups—a reminder that success is built on collective effort.

Crossing Symbolic Borders

As Die Welt noted, the location was symbolic—a direct reflection of Mainz 05's recent fall, yet brimming with potential to rise again. The second division was an opportunity, a chance to refine a craft that was less at the mercy of individual brilliance and more about teamwork.

Mainz's faith in Klopp never waned, with all season tickets sold out and corporate sponsorship pouring in for a new stadium. Yet, on the pitch, it was a time of change. With key players like Friedrich, Andreasen, and Zidan departed, new blood entered the team. Among them, Subotić emerged as a cornerstone, attributing his rapid development to Klopp's 'broad spectrum' of mentorship—a mix of old-school severity and supportive guidance that grew his talent.

Subotić speaks of Klopp's dual approach—firm but respectful, harsh but devoid of personal insult, a stark contrast to the often cutting nature of Bundesliga 2 coaching. Klopp's emotional intelligence, as observed by Doehling, was in understanding that one size does not fit all in management.

Mainz's season wavered between promising victories and stinging defeats, a mix that reflected the two sides of Klopp's team. Despite this, they remained in contention for promotion, and Klopp's reputation as a masterful coach only grew, piquing the interest of footballing powerhouses like Bayern Munich.

The Call from Bayern and the Road Not Taken

When Bayern's general manager, Uli Hoeness, dialled Klopp's number, it was a moment that could have changed his career. However, fate had different ideas, with Bayern opting for Jürgen Klinsmann instead. Though a blow, this choice inadvertently affirmed Klopp's coaching prowess on a national stage and perhaps, as history would reveal, spared him from a mismatched appointment.

Despite the flirtations of bigger clubs and a rollercoaster season, Klopp's heart seemed to be with Mainz. He had an emotional farewell. Tears flowed as Klopp, overwhelmed by the chorus of 'You'll Never Walk Alone', made his poignant exit, not as a defeated coach, but as a beloved figure whose impact was substantial.

# PART II:
# DORTMUND
# DREAMING

# CHAPTER 5: A NEW DAWN AT DORTMUND

## Appointment as Manager

When Klopp stepped into the role of Borussia Dortmund's manager, it was a moment deeply rooted in the club's struggles. Dortmund had been through a tough time, hovering in the lower half of the Bundesliga table. This was a far cry from their glorious history filled with championships. The devoted fans were hungry for a revival, yearning for the days when Dortmund was a football powerhouse.

Klopp's arrival brought a sense of hope that had been missing for too long. It wasn't just a change; it was a fresh start. Klopp had bigger plans than just bringing back the glory days. He carried an audacious vision to redefine the club's identity. He was all about attacking football and introducing "gegenpressing," a high-intensity pressing game. It wasn't just about winning; it was about entertaining the passionate Dortmund supporters.

Klopp's Vision

Jürgen Klopp's vision for Borussia Dortmund was groundbreaking and super ambitious. At its core was the aforementioned "gegenpressing," a tactical approach where the team pressed immediately to win back the ball when it was lost. It wasn't just a strategy; it was a style of play that demanded skill, hard work, and teamwork.

Klopp had a poetic way of describing it: "He likes having the ball, playing football, passes. It's like an orchestra. But it's a silent song. I like heavy metal." This was a big shift from the possession-based football others liked. Klopp wanted Dortmund to disrupt opponents, win the ball high up the pitch, and go for lightning-fast counter-attacks. This style resonated with fans and soon became Dortmund's trademark.

## Initial Challenges

But making Klopp's vision a reality was far from easy. Despite the excitement, he faced big challenges in the early days. The team had struggled in the Bundesliga, and Klopp inherited a squad that needed a total makeover. Turning Dortmund into a football powerhouse was going to take time, patience, and a ton of determination.

Klopp saw his team as "bows and arrows" compared to rivals like the mighty Bayern Munich, who had the financial resources of a "bazooka." He even joked, "The probability that they will hit the target is clearly higher. But then Robin Hood was apparently quite successful." This showed that Dortmund was the underdog, and Klopp fully embraced it. He was determined to build a team that could not only compete but also excel against the odds.

Dortmund's challenges were also made tougher by the financial gap between them and Bayern. But Klopp saw it as a challenge and welcomed the underdog role. He believed they could overcome the odds and build a team that could go head-to-head with the best in the league. His unwavering spirit became a source of inspiration for players and fans as they embarked on their remarkable journey to greatness.

## Gegenpressing: A Football Revolution

Gegenpressing, a cornerstone of Klopp's tactical philosophy, revolutionised football at Borussia Dortmund. This high-intensity strategy, as described by Hans-Joachim Watzke, CEO of Dortmund, was about playing "all-action football." Watzke observed that although they had very good players, not all were right for this demanding style, yet the team became more stable defensively under Klopp's guidance.

The core of gegenpressing is characterised by an intense approach to regain possession swiftly after losing it, requiring both physical fitness and mental resilience.

The success of gegenpressing hinges on teamwork and collective commitment. Peter Krawietz, Klopp's coaching assistant and chief scout, emphasised this, stating, "It's an agreement a team makes with itself. A social contract. 'Yes, we want to do that together.' One guy doing it by himself is nothing... That's why you need an agreement that's binding for everybody. "We will do it together, as soon as we lose the ball in the final third, we will try to win it back'".

Implementing gegenpressing is mentally and physically taxing. Players must decide whether to press again, even when fatigued, requiring synchronisation with teammates. Klopp's philosophy behind gegenpressing was based on exploiting the opponent's vulnerability at the moment of ball loss. "You have that moment where you have to overcome your inertia. Don't switch off. Don't be disappointed. The attack isn't over yet," Klopp advised, highlighting the psychological aspect of the tactic.

Ilkay Gündogan, reflecting on his time under Klopp at Dortmund, shared insights into the training emphasis on gegenpressing, "Klopp said the first one, two seconds after losing the ball, were decisive. We shouldn't be upset about losing the ball but actually be happy about being able to win it back. The idea was to attack the ball straight away, to surprise the opponent. They felt secure, they weren't ready for that".

Team Chemistry

Klopp's time at Borussia Dortmund was about more than just tactics and victories. It was about the incredible chemistry he built among his players. Beyond the tactics board, he had a unique talent for creating camaraderie, trust, and unity in his squad.

Klopp's charismatic personality was the foundation for this remarkable chemistry. One player fondly remembered, "Klopp had this aura that was truly magnetic. He made us believe that we were capable of achieving the impossible." Klopp's enthusiasm was infectious, and he instilled pride and purpose in his players.

When Klopp spoke, his players listened, not out of fear but out of respect and admiration. He wasn't just a coach; he was a mentor and friend. In times of doubt, he offered guidance and unwavering support.

## 2010/11 Season: Bundesliga Triumph

The 2010/11 season for Borussia Dortmund under Klopp was a defining moment in the club's history, marking their emergence as a dominant force in German football. Dortmund's success in this season can be attributed to Klopp's innovative tactics, diligently implemented by a team of young talents, inexpensive foreign players, and a few experienced heads. This blend created a potent collective force that not only upset the conventional order but also set new standards for football in the Bundesliga. His approach was particularly significant in a league that was losing its international prominence due to financial constraints and a culture of passive coaching. His strategy was seen as a way to enhance productivity using natural, renewable resources: a robust work ethic, humility, and cleverness.

The Italian national team's technical staff, led by coach Cesare Prandelli, visited Dortmund's training sessions, drawing comparisons to Arrigo Sacchi's AC Milan, a testament to the impact of Klopp's methodology. Klopp's ability to captivate and inspire players was evident in his interactions with new signings like İlkay Gündoğan, who was profoundly influenced by Klopp's honesty and approach to the game.

However, the season wasn't without its challenges. Dortmund struggled in the Champions League, failing to make an impact and finishing last in their group. This underperformance was attributed to a lack of experience, both in the squad and the coaching staff. The team's high-pressing style, so effective in the Bundesliga, was less successful on the European stage, where mistakes were more severely punished.

Despite these setbacks, Dortmund's domestic performance was nothing short of spectacular. From October 2011, the team embarked on a 28-game unbeaten run in the league. A crucial victory against Bayern Munich, their fourth consecutive win over the Bavarians, was pivotal in sealing the Bundesliga title. This success was underpinned by a perfect midfield positioning that created a 'kill zone' near the halfway line, disrupting Bayern's attacks.

Dortmund's players, united by shared hardships like the gruelling 'Chucky runs' set up by assistant coach Zeljko Buvac, developed a strong sense of camaraderie. This spirit was evident in their ability to turn games around, even after trailing. The team's dominance was such that they often overwhelmed their opponents, who were left helpless against Dortmund's relentless style.

The season culminated in Dortmund achieving their first-ever double, winning the league and the DFB-Pokal. Their cup run was marked by Klopp's motivational tactics, including showing the team edited highlights of historic wins. The final against Bayern Munich in Berlin was a masterclass, with Dortmund outplaying and humiliating their rivals in a 5-2 victory, a game that Klopp described as the "most extraordinary moment in [Borussia's] history".

This season firmly established Dortmund under Klopp as a force to be reckoned with in German football. Their approach not only brought success on the pitch but also changed the landscape of German football, challenging the traditional hegemony of clubs like Bayern Munich. The 2010/11 season will always be remembered as the time when Klopp and his Dortmund team grabbed the football world's attention with their passion, intensity, and revolutionary style of play.

## The Rocky Balboa Speech

In the pressurised world of football, managers are often expected to deliver rousing speeches that can inspire legions. But what happens when an epic speech falls flat? Klopp recounts one such story with a dose of humility.

He has always turned to the silver screen to find analogies for his team's journey—none more so than the underdog tale of Rocky Balboa. As he recounts his experience from 2011, it's clear that Klopp's intention was to instil a sense of belief in his Borussia Dortmund squad facing the colossus of Bayern Munich.

"I told them the truth of the situation: 'The last time Dortmund won in Munich, most of you were still in your Pampers,'" Klopp reminisces with a chuckle. His aim was to show that, like Rocky against Ivan Drago, they could overcome the odds, no matter how stacked against them.

Yet, the atmosphere took a turn when Klopp's cinematic references flew over the heads of his younger players. With most of his team unaware of the iconic boxer from Philly, the parallel he attempted to draw between Rocky's heart and Dortmund's spirit was lost in translation.

"Only two hands went up. Sebastian Kehl and Patrick Owomoyela," Klopp recalls the realisation hitting him, as he stood before a room of blank stares. Klopp chuckles, "We think we're giving the greatest speech in the history of football, and we're actually talking complete nonsense."

Klopp admits that the exact outcome of the match is lost to him. "I am pretty sure that I gave this speech in 2011 before we won 3–1," he speculates, though the victory isn't as memorable to him as that speech.

## Rise to Prominence

Under Klopp's leadership, Borussia Dortmund went on an incredible journey that took them to the top of German football. This rise wasn't just impressive; it was a defiance of the odds, a story that transcended borders, and a tale that captured the hearts of football fans far beyond Germany.

Winning the Bundesliga title was proof of Klopp's unwavering commitment to his football philosophy. Despite initial setbacks, he stayed determined. As he once joked, "During the first interview, I was very disappointed. During the second one, I already felt a bit better. If I wait half an hour, I'll probably have the feeling that we won." Klopp's belief in his vision was the driving force behind Dortmund's comeback.

Klopp wasn't just a manager; he was a visionary who transformed Dortmund's style of play. His philosophy wasn't just about winning; it was about winning with style. It was about capturing the essence of the beautiful game and infusing it with passion. Dortmund became known for high-intensity pressing, rapid counter-attacks, and an unquenchable desire to win.

## Wild Celebrations - The Night Klopp Painted the Town Yellow and Black

The Aftermath of Triumph

Klopp etched his name in Borussia Dortmund's history books, not just for clinching the Bundesliga title, but for the epic festivities that followed. The usually composed maestro of the pitch narrated a night so wild, it sounded more like fiction than the aftermath of a football campaign.

"I was really wasted which may have been noticeable in some interviews," Klopp confessed with the candour of a man who had nothing to hide. The partying had swept him away.

Klopp's recollection of the events after Dortmund's monumental victory was as confused as it was hilarious. "I actually woke up on a truck in the garage. All alone," he reminisced, a chuckle hidden in the confession.

As if waking up in a truck wasn't peculiar enough,

Klopp's night took another twist. "I walked across the yard and saw the silhouette of a man... it was Aki Watzke," Klopp said. It's almost comical, imagining the two figures — the football tactician and the club CEO — reunited in the vast emptiness of an industrial park.

Stranded and possibly still tipsy, Klopp and Watzke resorted to hitchhiking, a scene straight out of a buddy film. The Dortmund duo flagged down a driver, who initially refused to play chauffeur — that is until Watzke's offer of 200 euros persuaded him otherwise.

The journey, however, was far from ordinary. "I kept slamming my head into the side, I was a little tired," Klopp mused, only to discover the source of an odd clucking. "The trunk was full of..." his voice trailed off, leaving us to imagine Klopp's bemusement at finding himself a passenger in a makeshift poultry transport.

This adventure might seem crazy, but it is in keeping with a man who lives for moments of pure, unadulterated joy.

# CHAPTER 6: THE YELLOW WALL - AN UNBREAKABLE BOND

When Klopp took charge at Dortmund, he couldn't have anticipated the extraordinary bond he would build with the legendary Yellow Wall. This wasn't your ordinary stadium stand; it was a living, breathing entity that played a pivotal role in the team's success.

For Klopp, it was more than just a massive stand; it was a living, breathing force that could influence the team's performance. Dortmund's announcer, Norbert 'Nobby' Dickel, aptly described it, "The south stand has this unbelievable power; many opposing players are afraid of these people and this tremendous noise. When the game starts and the south stand sings, it's something very special. It's certainly the heart of BVB."

## The Powerhouse Südtribüne

The Südtribüne, fondly known as the Yellow Wall, was no ordinary stand; it was the very heart and soul of Borussia Dortmund. Measuring a staggering 328 feet in length and towering 131 feet high, it was a colossus of support.

It was designed to be truly remarkable. Originally

built for the 1974 FIFA World Cup, it expanded over the years. Dortmund's home ground, the Westfalenstadion, now stood as the largest stadium in Germany, capable of holding about 81,000 fervent fans.

Within the confines of this colossal stand, it didn't matter who you were. Doctors, teachers, students, grandparents, wives, and kids, all converged for one common purpose: to rally behind BVB. When Dortmund launched an attack or the opposition threatened, the Yellow Wall roared as one, exerting a profound influence on the game.

## Klopp's Profound Respect

Klopp held the Yellow Wall in the highest regard. His words capture the essence of the experience, "You come out, and the stadium explodes: out of the darkness and into the light. You look to your left, and it looks like 150,000 people are standing there, going crazy."

Teams facing Dortmund were wary of the Yellow Wall's might. Players from rival clubs could sense the intense energy emanating from this colossal stand. Bastian Schweinsteiger, a former star of Bayern Munich, openly confessed, "It's the Yellow Wall I'm most afraid of."

Klopp's words held immense weight with the fans, who, in turn, transformed the Yellow Wall into an impregnable fortress. Dortmund's goalkeeper,

Roman Weidenfeller, beautifully captured the essence of it, "If you are the enemy, it crushes you, but if you have her at your back as a goalkeeper, it's a fantastic feeling."

Klopp's time as coach will forever be entwined with the Yellow Wall, serving as a testament to the incredible power of unity and unwavering support in the beautiful game.

# CHAPTER 7: EUROPEAN ADVENTURES - THE RISE AND HEARTBREAK

## Dortmund's Unforgettable Champions League Journey

The 2012-2013 Champions League campaign marked a remarkable chapter in Borussia Dortmund's history, with Klopp at the helm, instilling belief into a side not considered among the favourites. This journey was a thrilling roller coaster.

"It's a very special club – a workers' club," Klopp reflected, emphasising the club's grassroots and community ethos. Dortmund transformed their fortress into a stage for some of their most unforgettable European nights, drawing strength from the 82,000 voices that roared in unison with every tackle, pass, and goal.

Memorable Victories and the 'Group of Death'

The group stage was a testament to Klopp's genius, navigating through the treacherous 'Group of Death' with Manchester City, Real Madrid, and Ajax. Dortmund emerged undefeated, with Klopp's system proving resilient against Europe's elite, offering a glimpse of the remarkable journey that lay ahead.

Despite the departures of key players like Shinji Kagawa, Dortmund's resolve remained unwavering. Klopp's philosophy transcended tactics; it was about fostering emotional unity, encouraging his players to treasure every moment on the pitch. "This is what you should always feel – until you die," he passionately conveyed.

Thrilling Knockout Stages

The knockout phases pushed Dortmund's spirit to its limits. A dramatic comeback against Malaga in the quarterfinals embodied their campaign's spirit – unyielding, relentless, and driven by heart. The Westfalenstadion witnessed two stoppage-time goals that kept their European dream alive, a miracle that was part of Klopp's design and part of the players' indomitable will.

Then came the momentous semi final against Real

Madrid. Klopp was well aware of the enormity of the challenge. "We need to work seriously and sensibly," he said, alluding to Dortmund's approach against the financial giants of football.

## The Semifinal Triumph: Dortmund vs. Madrid

On the grandest of stages, a David-versus-Goliath narrative unfolded. Borussia Dortmund, orchestrated by Klopp, faced the Herculean task of toppling the indomitable Real Madrid. Klopp, however, with foresight in his eyes, devised a plan to challenge and unseat the giants from their throne.

Revisiting this clash, Klopp's recounting revealed a battle strategy well-executed. "It was about tactical adjustments," Klopp admitted. His blueprint revolved around an element of surprise, shifting focus to areas on the pitch rarely exploited against the Spanish giants.

The first leg of the semifinals saw Dortmund execute a plan that was audacious as it was effective. "We overloaded the left," Klopp later revealed, targeting the flank guarded by none other than Cristiano Ronaldo, exploiting his forward forays that often left gaps in his wake.

Lewandowski's Heroics and Dortmund's Triumph

The spotlight shone undeniably on Robert Lewandowski. The Polish striker became the embodiment of Klopp's tactical brilliance. His four-goal haul left the Madrid defence, often deemed impenetrable, in disarray.

"And Mario Götze played man-marking against Alonso!" Klopp highlighted, underscoring the duel that effectively disrupted Madrid's rhythm. Alonso, often the conductor of Madrid's midfield, found himself shadowed by Götze, his influence stifled, his usual orchestration muted under Dortmund's tactical spell.

A stunning 4-1 victory was as much a triumph of the mind as it was of the game. The tactical nuance, the audacious game plan, and individual brilliance converged in a harmony that not only overcame but overwhelmed José Mourinho's star-studded side.

The Night That Shook Football

As the final whistle blew, it was evident that Klopp's Dortmund had not just defeated Real Madrid; they had delivered a footballing masterclass that would be talked about for years. It was a night where David met Goliath and won – not by sheer force, but by the artistry of mind and motion, a match that would live long in the memory of those who witnessed it.

## The Heartbreak of the 2013 Final

Beneath the evening sky of London, Wembley Stadium witnessed the dreams of a team that had captured the footballing world's imagination. The final was not just a clash of two German titans but a tale of two philosophies, with Klopp's high-octane, gegenpressing machine pitted against the tactically disciplined Bayern Munich, poised for European glory. As Dortmund's fans, draped in yellow and black, sang with an intensity reverberating around the stadium, the team responded on the pitch with a fervour that matched their supporters'.

The match ebbed and flowed, with Dortmund throwing everything they had into the game. In the first 25 minutes, they ignited hopes, but Mats Hummels lamented, "We were the better team... but we missed the goal we needed." The intensity was palpable; every pass, tackle, and shot carried the weight of history and the dreams of thousands.

The Decisive Moment

With the teams level at 1-1, then came the moment that tilted the balance - in the 89th minute - when Arjen Robben, a player redeemed from previous year's agony, danced through the defence to score the winner. "It was a free-kick, and we were not in the right formation," Klopp recounted, the weariness of a season that demanded every drop of their spirit evident in his voice.

Despite the defeat, Klopp's pride in his team was unmistakable. "But we deserved to be in the final, and we showed that tonight." It was an acknowledgment of their journey, their fight, and the sheer will.

Reflections

For Klopp, the match was a narrative woven into

footballing lore. "We are a club, not a company," he mused, presenting Dortmund as the embodiment of the pure, beating heart of football—a sentiment that resonated deeply with the neutral fan who longs for the romance of the underdog.

In the days that followed, Dortmund's players and fans licked their wounds. It was a loss that cut deep, a pain only those who had come so close to glory could understand. Yet, within the heartache, there was a flicker of pride, an awareness that they had dared to dream, dared to disrupt the hierarchy of European football.

# CHAPTER 8: FAREWELL TO DORTMUND - KLOPP'S EMOTIONAL DEPARTURE

## The Storm Before The Calm

The 2014/15 season was the storm that no forecast could have predicted. The summer preceding the fateful season was a mixed bag, a mingling of optimism and looming troubles. Dortmund's preseason was promising, with victories that made fans dream big, despite losing Lewandowski to the clutches of Bayern. They even bested the Bavarian giants to lift the Supercup, with the crowd at Signal Iduna Park roaring in approval. But there was an undercurrent of unease; the heavy defeat to Liverpool in preseason was jarring—the first hint of a tough season ahead.

## Cracks in the Armor

The opening day disaster—a goal conceded in mere seconds against Leverkusen—was a crack that would widen with time. Klopp's army was without its generals—Hummels, Gundogan, Sahin, and Blaszczykowski were all sidelined. It was a foreshadowing of the trials that lay ahead, a test of depth and resolve for a side used to punching above their weight.

The injury plague seemed relentless, and as the weeks rolled on, the missing faces on the pitch began to tell a story of a campaign cursed with setbacks. Even the return of key players like Hummels couldn't reverse the fortunes. The Derby loss to Schalke left fans and players alike in a state of shell-shocked reflection—where had the Dortmund that dazzled Europe gone?

## In Klopp We Trust... But for How Long?

As autumn leaves fell, so did Dortmund's points tally. A succession of losses in October had the pundits chattering and the Yellow Wall rumbling with discontent. Yet, through this storm, the unwavering support for Klopp stood firm. The man who had engineered Dortmund's renaissance was now tasked with its salvage operation. His response? A candid admission of the need to work harder, to strive through the adversities.

November brought glimpses of hope—a narrow victory against Gladbach was a brief respite. Yet, as Dortmund slumped to the depths of the table, Klopp's resolve was put to the test. The fans began to show their discontent, yet Klopp understood.

The Darkest Hour

As the winter chill set in, Klopp's words echoed with defiance: "We didn't become stupid overnight." The team still knew how to win, but the question was—when? December saw a squad inching towards full strength, with Sahin and Blaszczykowski returning to the team. Yet, victories were sparse, and the Champions League campaign was on thin ice. The year ended with a Dortmund side unfamiliar to many—an ensemble of brilliance struggling to find their tune.

The Phoenix Rises... Briefly

Then came the resurgence, as Klopp had prophesied. The new year began with hiccups, but soon, the wins piled up. February saw a contract extension for Reus, a statement of faith, a commitment to the cause. The team clawed their way up the table, and Klopp's conviction seemed to be paying dividends. But was this uptick in form a false dawn?

The Last Dance

As the end drew near, so did the vultures, circling

around the legacy Klopp had built. March's fickle form, the Champions League farewell, and the domestic slip-ups were heavy blows.

## An Unexpected Announcement

As the 2014/15 football season neared its end, Dortmund and its devoted fans stood at the brink of an emotional transition. When Klopp approached the microphone at the press conference, a palpable sense of anticipation hung in the air. With a tremor in his voice that betrayed his typically stoic demeanour, he confirmed the swirling rumours – he was stepping down. The announcement sent shockwaves through the football world. Klopp wasn't just a coach; he had been the visionary behind Dortmund's dreams, guiding them to glorious heights with consecutive Bundesliga triumphs, a DFB Cup victory, and a Champions League final that had thrilled fans around the world.

Reasons for Departure

It wasn't the mere reflection of their place in the league table, not the shadow of a disappointing tenth place, that had driven Klopp's decision. It was something deeper, a culmination of moments leading to an inevitable crossroads. Football, with its relentless pace, had brought Klopp to a juncture where he believed the path forward for Dortmund was one he could no longer lead.

Addressing the gathered crowd, Klopp's words resonated with the profound bond he shared with Dortmund. "No one needs to be grateful to me," he said, every syllable soaked in emotion. "We've lived a fairy tale, but even the best stories have their last page." His final hope was simple – to bid farewell to Dortmund on a high, with one more celebration, one more triumphant moment atop a truck at Borsigplatz.

Klopp dismissed whispers of exhaustion and speculation of a sabbatical. "This is a time when planning for the new season begins," he emphasised, making it clear that his departure was a thoughtful decision for the club's long-term prosperity.

## Farewell Messages

Sentiments expressed by Hans-Joachim Watzke

resonated with the respect and camaraderie they had built. "It was an extremely difficult decision for us," Watzke confessed, the weight of the decision heavy on hearts steeped in friendship and mutual success.

Michael Zorc's tribute spoke volumes of the legacy left behind. "Jürgen Klopp has helped write history," Zorc acknowledged, crediting Klopp with the club's resurgence. Zorc's call for a proper send-off was a rallying cry for everyone who bled yellow and black – to honour a man who had given them so much.

Klopp's Legacy

The Klopp era was one of transformation – a journey from Bundesliga regulars to European titans. The legacy he left behind was massive in the silverware and the memories, but it was his spirit that truly transformed Dortmund.

The task of filling his shoes seemed monumental. Dortmund wasn't just searching for a new coach; they were seeking someone who could carry on a legacy. The question of Klopp's next destination lingered, with the football world eagerly awaiting to see where the man who rejuvenated Dortmund would work his magic next.

His departure marked the end of an era, but not the end of his influence. As he ventured into new horizons, one thing was certain – Jürgen Klopp's story was far from over. The footballing world watched with bated breath as Klopp prepared to take his next step.

# PART III: THE ANFIELD ODYSSEY

# CHAPTER 9: THE KOP AWAITS - KLOPP'S ARRIVAL AT ANFIELD

## The Buzz Begins

October 8, 2015. Liverpool fans were gripped by a wave of excitement. The air was thick with anticipation. Rumours had been swirling, and the name on everyone's lips was Jürgen Klopp. The German maestro, known for his football alchemy at Borussia Dortmund, was set to land on Merseyside. It was more than a buzz; it was an electric charge through the heart of Liverpool.

Journalists were in a frenzy, the echo of typing and phone calls filled newsrooms – Klopp's potential arrival was the headline in waiting. "The story of the week," Carl Markham of the Press Association remembered, describing the feverish hunt for any tidbit that would confirm Klopp as the new

Reds' skipper. "Everyone was on the case," he added, painting a picture of the media circus that unfolded.

At 3.44pm CEST, a plane left Dortmund for John Lennon Airport. Little did anyone know, over 35,000 pairs of eyes would follow its journey online. This wasn't just any flight; it was carrying hope, excitement, and the future of Liverpool FC in the form of Klopp. The air-traffic site flightradar24's servers were buzzing; this was a pivotal moment where football and technology intertwined like never before.

3.58pm on Thursday, an email dropped, veiled in secrecy yet obvious in intent. It spoke of a press conference for a "major club announcement." Speculations raced – could this be it?

By 8.58pm, the cat was out of the bag. Social media was ablaze with the news – Klopp was officially at the helm of Liverpool FC. The world waited with bated breath for his vision for the club. His first proclamation as boss? A call to transform "from doubters to believers."

Come 10am Friday, the press had congregated, eager for Klopp's first address. The 'Reds Lounge' was packed to the rafters, journalists jostling for a glimpse of Liverpool's new leader. Klopp took to the stage, his presence magnetic.

The press conference room was charged with anticipation, with reporters from across the globe eagerly waiting for Klopp to take the podium. His magnetic presence was undeniable, and his reputation as a footballing visionary had preceded him.

## 'The Normal One'

When questioned about how he would describe himself compared to Jose Mourinho's claim of being the 'special one,' Klopp's response evoked laughter. "I don't want to describe myself. Does anyone in this room think I can do wonders? No? I'm a very normal guy," he said with a grin. "I came from the Black Forest, and my mother may be sitting in front of the TV, watching this press conference and has said no word until now. But she is very proud. So I'm the totally normal guy.

I'm the normal one, maybe, if you want this..."

'The normal one' moniker would soon become an endearing symbol of Klopp's humility and authenticity. He even had a coffee mug emblazoned with "The Normal One," serving as a subtle reminder that despite the grandeur of the stage, Klopp remained grounded, a down-to-earth figure poised to lead Liverpool into a new era.

Markham reflected on Klopp's linguistic prowess, his ability to read a room and command respect with both wit and wisdom. "There doesn't appear to be any question he won't answer," Markham noted, highlighting Klopp's openness and the personable nature of his interactions.

## The Weight of History

When Klopp took the helm at Liverpool, the club had endured a 25-year wait for a league title. The pressure was immense, both internally and externally. Klopp offered a brilliant analogy to encapsulate this pressure, one he would revisit throughout his early years at Liverpool. He likened the weight of the club's history to a backpack that couldn't be carried indefinitely. "Twenty-five years ago, it's a long time," Klopp mused. "All this time, people have strived to improve and to secure the next title. History is the foundation for us, but we can't carry our illustrious past around like a burden in a backpack."

Klopp's message was clear: while the past held significance, it should not shackle progress. The weight of history could not be borne indefinitely; it was time to set it aside and look forward.

The Prediction

Klopp did not shy away from making a bold prediction on that first day. He proclaimed, "This could be a truly special day if you want it to be and if you work for it and if you are patient enough. We start today in a challenging league against increasingly formidable opponents, but in a unique Liverpool way, we can achieve success. We can't say we have to wait for 20 years, but when I sit here in four years, I'm pretty sure we will have won a title."

The room brimmed with determination. Klopp's words weren't empty promises; they were a call to action. Fans and players alike clung to those words as Klopp's Liverpool embarked on an incredible journey. It was a journey that would ultimately culminate in both the Champions League and the long-awaited Premier League title, fulfilling Klopp's prophecy.

## 'Full Throttle Football'

Klopp's footballing philosophy was crystal clear from the outset. He pledged 'full throttle football,' characterised by passion, emotion, and relentless energy. "Everyone knows me; it's about emotion, it's about speed. All the things that make football interesting for me, I want to see on the pitch," he declared. "In this era, we will have to earn points and win games without promising a particular style of football. I once said 'full throttle football' in Dortmund, but, goodness, I cannot repeat the same words forever. But it will be 'full throttle football.'"

Under Klopp, Liverpool wholeheartedly embraced this style of play. The Anfield faithful were treated to exhilarating matches brimming with passion and excitement. It was a brand of football that mirrored Klopp's own personality – intense, energetic, and unrelenting. 'Full throttle football' wasn't just a pledge; it was a commitment to entertain and succeed.

Perhaps the most enduring quote from that day was Klopp's call for a shift in mindset. "You have to change from a doubter to a believer. We have to begin anew, and then we'll see what happens this year." Klopp's arrival marked not just a shift in footballing philosophy but a transformation in the hearts and minds of everyone associated with Liverpool Football Club.

His words served as a rallying cry, a challenge to alter perspectives and embrace a new era. The doubters had to become believers.

## The Klopp Effect Begins

Klopp's entry into Liverpool came with a tidal wave of expectation. Fans were pining for the sort of success that the club had tasted in the past, and Klopp, with his track record, seemed like the man to lead this charge.

Klopp's Liverpool was inconsistent yet promising. There were spectacular moments, like the 4-1 victory against Manchester City in November that had fans dreaming big. But there were also setbacks, such as the 2-0 loss to Newcastle in December, showing that Klopp's project was still a work in progress.

His influence started to take hold as Liverpool demolished Aston Villa 6-0 in February, but his Reds also fell to a 3-2 defeat against Southampton after leading 2-0. It was a rollercoaster, with every high followed by a learning curve, but it was thrilling, nonetheless.

The Europa League journey felt like a throwback to European nights of old. There was the remarkable 2-0 win against Manchester United in March, which set the stage for the unforgettable comeback against Borussia Dortmund in April, overturning a 3-1 deficit to win 4-3 on an electrifying night at Anfield.

## The West Brom Celebration

Liverpool were grappling with West Brom, trying to eke out a win. The game had its ups and downs, with the Reds falling behind to the Baggies before battling back. As the match looked to be slipping away, up popped Divock Origi with a deflected shot in the dying embers of stoppage time, making it 2-2. The crowd erupted, and the manager? Well, Klopp went wild on the touchline, his glasses nearly taking flight in the excitement.

But the drama didn't end with the final whistle. In a move that had everyone talking, Klopp gathered his players and led them to The Kop for a unified, arms-raised salute to the fans - after a 2-2 home draw with West Brom! It certainly raised more than a few eyebrows in the media and rival fans.

After the game, when the adrenaline had settled just a bit, Klopp explained his actions. "I really wanted from the first day that the people know about their importance," he said, keen on acknowledging the fans' role in Liverpool's performance.

And so, even though some rival fans and players didn't get it—James McClean notably called him "a bit of an idiot"—Klopp stood firm on his intentions. To him, it was crystal clear: "Why should we even discuss that?"

Klopp, with his trademark enthusiasm, was eager to lay down the foundations of what he envisions for Liverpool. "I wanted to show that we really are one unit, 100 percent one unit," he explained. "It's still very different routines in England and in Germany," he acknowledged, but stood by his belief that such moments of unity are important.

His mission was clear: to make Anfield a fortress where the fans are as much a part of the game as the players on the pitch. "There is no limit to what we can do actually," Klopp said. "This is a fantastic moment to be a Liverpudlian, because it's all so positive in a not-so-positive world," he reflected.

## Basel Heartbreak - The 2015/16 Europa League Final

The first 45 minutes in Basel saw Liverpool lead Sevilla through a Daniel Sturridge beauty, his outside-of-the-boot finish curling into the far corner. The Reds looked to be in control, marching towards what seemed to be a triumphant end to Klopp's first campaign.

But football is a game of two halves, and Sevilla demonstrated that with a swift and crushing turnaround. The Spanish side's equaliser came just 17 seconds into the second half. As Klopp remarked later, "We lost faith in our style of play... We changed from passing simply and quickly to complicated. We lost our formation."

Klopp's Post-Match Reflections

In the aftermath, Klopp was candid, his quotes reflecting both his analytical mind and passionate heart. "It was obvious the first goal of Sevilla had a big influence on our game... The first half was OK, and we deserved the 1-0 lead," he said, acknowledging Liverpool's initial control.

Klopp noted the psychological impact the equaliser had on his team: "In this moment we lost faith in our style of play... Everything changed in this moment."

But true to his nature, Klopp looked to the future, seeing the defeat not as an end but a beginning: "Now it's clear we are not in a European competition next year... it means we have time to train. We will use it, and we will come back stronger, that's for sure."

He emphasised the necessity of growing from the experience: "Now we are disappointed and frustrated, 100 percent. Tomorrow, in a week or whatever we will see it a little bit more clearly and then we will use this experience... Basel was a very decisive moment for the wonderful future of Liverpool FC."

Klopp didn't shy away from self-criticism and recognized his role in the team's reaction to adversity: "I saw it, so I tried to change it but... It's all about us, it's all about me. It's my job to help the players react better in different situations, so I can improve a lot."

He looked firmly towards the next season, highlighting the importance of preparation and learning: "We will do something with transfers, that's clear. But, first of all, we need to use the experience because I am sure we will be in a final again."

Post-Basel and the Promise

Even in the shadow of the loss, Klopp's resolve was unwavering, and his vision for Liverpool's future remained crystal clear. He closed on an optimistic note, knowing the journey was just beginning: "I have a lot of luck in my life that I sit here and I am the manager of Liverpool FC... we will carry on and I will carry on."

The 2015/16 season was a bumpy yet exhilarating ride, a prelude to the Klopp era that promised highs, lows, and above all, memorable football. Liverpool under Klopp had shown glimmers of brilliance and, with the wisdom gleaned from

Basel's heartache, the stage was set for a comeback.

## Klopp's Reds Rise - The 2016/17 Season

The onset of the 2016/17 season heralded a period of electric performances by Liverpool, characterised by a stunning 4-3 victory over Arsenal. This match set the stage for Liverpool's dynamic and aggressive approach under Klopp's leadership. Despite the exhilarating start, the team faced a setback with a 2-0 loss to Burnley. Klopp's reaction was analytical and forward-looking:

"We had about 80 percent possession... But there are different ways to play football, that's absolutely OK... we win, if we don't make mistakes in the wrong moment. But we did. Now we have to accept the result and carry on.".

Tough Lessons and Tactical Shifts

Liverpool faced a significant challenge when Sadio Mane left for the Africa Cup of Nations. Mane's speed and skill were crucial to the Reds' attack, and his absence was keenly felt. Klopp, known for his adaptability, had to reconfigure his squad. He acknowledged the impact of the departure, remarking, "Can we play exactly the same football? Probably not, but who cares. We play the football we are able to play then, that's the situation". This period was tough for Liverpool, as they struggled to replicate the form shown with Mane in the team. Klopp was candid about the situation, admitting, "You can't always have the perfect solution. In this case, it's absolutely far away from being perfect without these players. But we knew it, and now we have to deal with it". His words underscored the difficulty of the moment but also his resolve to push through and find success with the resources at hand.

Big Games and Big Moments

One of the standout wins was against city rivals Everton. The Reds triumphed 3-1 in a game that saw Sadio Mane's clinical finishing, Coutinho's genius strike from 40 yards, and Origi's immediate impact off the bench with a powerful finish. This derby victory was a defining moment, strengthening Liverpool's top-four bid.

Another significant victory came against Watford, with Liverpool putting six past the visitors. Mane's header opened the scoring, followed by Coutinho and Can's goals to secure a 3-0 lead at half-time. The relentless Reds added two more via Firmino and Mane, and despite Watford pulling one back, Wijnaldum's injury-time goal sealed the resounding 6-1 victory, the highest scored by Liverpool that season.

Liverpool's 3-1 win over Arsenal was another critical moment for their Champions League ambitions. The Reds delivered a dominant performance with Firmino and Mane scoring in the first half. Despite Arsenal's efforts to come back into the game, Wijnaldum's late strike ensured victory and sent the Anfield crowd into ecstasy.

Ending on a High

The season culminated in Liverpool securing Champions League qualification, a testament to the hard work and progress made under Klopp. The final game against Middlesbrough was a pivotal moment. After two disappointing results, Liverpool returned to winning ways with Origi and Lallana providing goals, lifting the team to second place in the table. Klopp's decision-making, particularly in goalkeeping, was evident as he justified the replacement of Karius with Mignolet, underscoring his focus on managing player pressure and seizing opportunities.

Reflecting on the season's journey and looking to the future, Klopp remained optimistic, stating, "It was not too bad so far, let's try to make it even better in the future." This encapsulated the ethos of a team ready to take on greater challenges and continue building their legacy.

# CHAPTER 10: BUILDING THE TEAM - KLOPP'S VISION FOR LIVERPOOL

## Reinventing the Squad

Klopp's tenure at Liverpool was marked by his unwavering commitment to crafting a team that could conquer the footballing world. His vision for the squad was clear, and he pursued it with zest. Among the gems he unearthed was Sadio Mane, a player whose potential had caught Klopp's eye long before he arrived at Anfield.

Klopp's admiration for Mane's talents was apparent as he reflected, "I've been following Sadio for many years, starting with his impressive performances in the 2012 Olympics, and then observing his growth in Austria and during his time at Southampton." It was this astute eye for talent that made Mane a top priority for Liverpool during the summer of 2016.

The Liverpool manager engaged extensively with his coaching staff, discussing Mane's potential impact on the team. Klopp remarked, "Since my arrival, I've had many discussions with the staff about him, always believing that he could be a fantastic addition to our squad." In Mane, Klopp saw a player of exceptional quality, blessed with a strong work ethic and an impressive goal-scoring record—a perfect match for his vision of Liverpool's future.

But Klopp's interest in Mane extended beyond his footballing prowess. Klopp emphasised, "During our conversations, I could sense his deep desire to be part of our club and to perform in front of our incredible fans." Klopp understood that this passion would resonate strongly with the Liverpool faithful.

Timing was of the essence, and Klopp and his team executed the transfer to ensure that Mane could be an integral part of the squad from the very first day of pre-season training. This strategic move provided Liverpool with a significant advantage, enabling Mane to seamlessly integrate into Klopp's tactical plans and the team's preparations for the upcoming season.

## The Klopp Effect on Young Talents

Klopp has always been much more than just a manager to his players. Jordon Ibe's words resonate with this sentiment perfectly. Back in December 2015, Ibe was a bright-eyed 20-year-old thriving under the wings of Klopp. He brought out a side of Klopp that we often sense but rarely get such a clear view of. "He's cool, you know?" Ibe said, shedding light on how Klopp builds one-on-one relationships with his players, fostering respect and camaraderie, crucial for any player's development.

What stands out is the trust and freedom Klopp instils in his youngsters. He's not the gaffer who will give you an earful for losing the ball, provided you show the grit to win it back. That's pure Klopp – a manager who cares less about mistakes and more about the response to those mistakes. And this isn't just for the experienced heads in the team.

## Preparing for the Challenge

Klopp's commitment to constructing a formidable squad extended beyond signing players like Mane. He was determined to prepare his team meticulously for the formidable challenges that awaited them. Klopp stressed the critical role of pre-season preparations as he meticulously designed an intensive training regimen for his squad.

The Liverpool manager recognized that peak physical fitness would be pivotal to the club's aspirations in the demanding Premier League. He spared no effort in ensuring that his players were in the best possible shape. Klopp revealed his plans for a tough schedule of triple training sessions, a testament to his unwavering dedication to elevating the squad's fitness levels.

As Mane joined the Liverpool ranks, he conveyed his enthusiasm for the upcoming pre-season preparations, emphasising his eagerness to collaborate with his new teammates. "Starting late in pre-season isn't easy, but I've signed today, and I'm ready to join the team immediately," declared Mane. His determination to contribute to the collective effort and make a positive impact in his debut season at Liverpool was palpable.

With Mane's arrival, Klopp had at his disposal an array of attacking talents, including the likes of Adam Lallana, Roberto Firmino, Philippe Coutinho, and Lazar Markovic. The competition for a spot in the starting lineup was fierce, but it was a challenge that Klopp wholeheartedly embraced.

The manager's philosophy was unequivocal: he desired a squad brimming with quality players who could motivate each other to reach new heights. Klopp's faith in Mane and his meticulous approach to shaping the team were unmistakable, setting the stage for a season filled with promise and excitement.

# CHAPTER 11: 'HEAVY METAL' FOOTBALL - KLOPP'S TACTICAL REVOLUTION

In the intricate world of football tactics, where managers often obsess over possession and precise passing, Klopp was a breath of fresh air with his approach that came to be known as 'heavy metal' football. While Europe was enamoured by the possession game of Pep Guardiola's Barcelona, Klopp found himself drawn to a different aspect of the beautiful game. It wasn't the passing carousel that most interested him; it was the relentless pursuit of winning the ball back.

Klopp's admiration for Barcelona's pressing game was evident, "It's extraordinary how high up the pitch this team is when they win the ball back. And the reason they do that is because every player presses." He saw in their tenacity a reflection of his own footballing philosophy—a philosophy that would go on to change the way teams approached the game.

## The Art of Winning the Ball Back

Gegenpressing wasn't just about countering an opponent's press; it was about initiating a press of their own, instantly winning back possession when the ball was lost. His Dortmund side was designed to excel in this approach, and Klopp believed it was a potent attacking weapon.

"Gegenpressing lets you win back the ball nearer to the goal," Klopp explained. He understood that it took just one pass from regaining possession to creating a golden goal-scoring opportunity. In Klopp's eyes, no playmaker in the world could match the effectiveness of a well-executed gegenpressing situation, making it a vital component of his tactical blueprint.

## Creating Space Through Gegenpressing

While many managers were fixated on vertical compactness, Klopp paid equal attention to horizontal compactness in his gegenpressing strategy. He recognized that compressing space quickly was key to its success, and his wide midfielders played a pivotal role in achieving this. They would tuck inside, effectively boxing the opposition towards the touchline, limiting their options and facilitating the gegenpressing.

Klopp's gegenpressing philosophy wasn't just about winning the ball back; it was a systematic approach that reshaped football tactics. His influence extended far beyond Germany, and the term "Gegenpressing" became widely recognized in football circles.

Liverpool fans embraced the relentless energy and passion with which their team played. It wasn't just football; it was a spectacle—a high-octane, full-throttle style that had fans on the edge of their seats, cheering for every press, every tackle, and every counter-attack.

## Semi-Final Glory

In the spring of 2018, Liverpool faced AS Roma in the UEFA Champions League semi-finals. This encounter, held on April 24, 2018, at Anfield, was set against the backdrop of Liverpool's impressive journey filled with exhilarating attacking football. The first leg is especially memorable for Liverpool's explosive performance, largely credited to Mohamed Salah, who was facing his former team. Salah's two stunning goals and two assists were pivotal, showcasing his top form. His first goal, a beautifully curled shot, set the tone for the match. Sadio Mane and Roberto Firmino added to the damage, with Firmino scoring twice, propelling Liverpool to a 5-0 lead by the 68th minute. However, Roma managed a late comeback with goals from Edin Dzeko and Diego Perotti, hinting at a possible turnaround in the second leg.

The return leg in Rome, held on May 2, 2018,

at the Stadio Olimpico, was a nerve-wracking affair for Liverpool. Despite an early setback caused by an own goal from James Milner and a goal from Dzeko, Liverpool responded with goals from Wijnaldum and Mane. However, Roma did not back down easily, scoring two late goals. Despite Roma's valiant efforts, Liverpool emerged victorious with an aggregate score of 7-6, a testament to their formidable performance in the first leg at Anfield.

Klopp's tactical prowess was a significant factor in these matches. His strategy of high pressing, quick transitions, and utilising the lethal trio of Salah, Mane, and Firmino overwhelmed Roma. The use of full-backs to create width and the midfield's role in tempo control were also crucial to Liverpool's success.

This semi-final victory was significant for Liverpool, marking their return to the top tier of European football. Salah's performance across both legs highlighted his exceptional talent and was a key factor in Liverpool's success. The high-scoring drama of the tie, culminating in a 7-6 aggregate score, remains one of the most thrilling in recent Champions League history. Although Liverpool faced a final hurdle against Real Madrid, this campaign marked the beginning of a golden era for the club, re-establishing them as a powerhouse in European football.

## Klopp's Reaction

Klopp's post-match press conference was a blend of overwhelming pride and a touch of realism. Reflecting on the Reds' journey to the final, he was visibly moved by the achievement. He highlighted the team's progression from a qualifier to reaching the final, emphasising his happiness for the players, the club, and the fans. Klopp remarked on the fantastic ride the team had experienced so far and expressed excitement about heading to Kiev for the final, a statement that underscored the remarkable nature of their achievement.

His reaction was not just about celebration; he also brought a sense of realism to the occasion. Drawing upon Liverpool's previous experiences in cup finals during his tenure, he emphasised the importance of not just reaching finals but winning them. "Going to a final is really nice—I did it a few times—but winning it is even nicer. We will be ready," he stated, indicating a forward-looking approach towards the upcoming challenge in Kiev.

The Liverpool manager also didn't lose sight of the Premier League responsibilities, with a significant match against Chelsea on the horizon. He balanced the euphoria of European success with the need for continued focus in the domestic league. Additionally, Klopp commented on Sadio Mane's defining performance in the semi-final, acknowledging his importance to the team while playfully noting that it wasn't his best performance for the club.

## The Night in Kiev

Klopp's team was ready to face the titans of Real Madrid in Kiev. The Champions League final - the pinnacle of European club football - was the stage set.

## The Boxer Shorts Story

It was the eve of the final—a night of high stakes and frayed nerves. Yet within the confines of the Liverpool camp, the atmosphere took an unexpected turn. Gini Wijnaldum, Liverpool's midfield dynamo at the time, shared a gem of a story that perfectly encapsulates Klopp's unique approach to management.

Before the biggest game of their season, instead of a stern, tense talk, Klopp chose a different tactic. "He did the meeting with his shirt stuffed inside his 'CR7' boxers," Wijnaldum recalled, a chuckle almost audible in his voice. "The whole changing room was on the floor laughing their heads off."

This wasn't just a random act of silliness; it was Klopp's calculated move to dissolve tension, a psychological pat on the back to his players saying, "Relax, we've got this." He was providing a moment of levity in the face of immense pressure —something Klopp seems to have a natural flair for.

Wijnaldum continued, "Usually, in those situations, everyone is serious and concentrated. But he was relaxed and made this joke." It speaks volumes of Klopp's philosophy. As he has been quoted saying, "I am not a dreamer. I am a football romantic."

Klopp's ability to remain poised and even inject humour into the most pressure-cooker situations is a testament to his leadership. His confidence, often worn as casually as those Ronaldo-branded boxers, is infectious. "If you see that your manager is really confident and relaxed, it will have an effect on players," Wijnaldum observed.

## Salah's Injury: A Shattered Dream

"Of course it was a big moment in the game," Klopp recounted, the wound still fresh, reflecting on the incident that shifted the tides. Mohamed Salah, Liverpool's talisman, clashed with Sergio Ramos and came off worse, his shoulder bearing the brunt of a fall. "It's like wrestling a little bit and it's unlucky then that Mo fell on his shoulder," Klopp remarked, reflecting on the agony of the moment.

The Shift in Momentum

In the aftermath, there was a noticeable shift. The confidence of the Reds was shaken as their star man left the field, tears streaming down his face. "The shock of the boys was obvious," Klopp admitted. Real Madrid, seasoned in these battles, sensed the opportunity, pressing forward, seeking to capitalise on the sudden vulnerability in Liverpool's armour.

Gareth Bale's introduction was a stroke of genius from Zinedine Zidane. The Welshman executed an unbelievable bicycle kick, a moment tilted the game in Madrid's favour. "It was a fantastic goal, an unbelievable goal," Klopp praised.

Luck seemed to have deserted Liverpool, a sentiment echoed by Klopp. "We not only had no luck – we had none plus bad luck," he mused. A deflected shot, a pair of goalkeeping errors from Loris Karius, and the ball hitting the woodwork, all moments that could have swung in favour of Liverpool on another day, conspired against them.

"It's very bad for Mo, very bad for us, and very

bad for Egypt," Klopp said, acknowledging the bad news Salah's injury represented. "That's part of the sport," he sighed.

## Resilience in Defeat

The game continued with Liverpool attempting to salvage pride, to find a way back, but the night was unforgiving. "We were there, we were here, we did the things we are good in," said Klopp, his pride in his team's performance and ethos unshaken by the defeat.

The spotlight fell on Loris Karius, whose errors had been critical. "I have only very, very few words after the game but it's nothing to talk about," Klopp mentioned, a gesture of solidarity towards his goalkeeper. "We will be with him, there's no doubt about that."

The defeat was raw, and Klopp did not hide his emotions. "I'm the opposite of fine," he confessed, embodying the collective despair of the Liverpool faithful.

Acceptance and Hope

As the final whistle blew, sealing a 3-1 victory for Real Madrid, the Reds' hearts sank. The journey to the summit had ended just short of glory. "I did the best I could and it was not good enough, and I have to accept that, that's it," Klopp reflected somberly.

Despite the defeat, Klopp's belief in his team, in their style of play, and in the ethos that had brought them to the final remained unwavering. As they walked off the pitch, Klopp and his men knew that their journey wasn't over. It was merely the beginning of another challenge, another fight, another day to strive for greatness.

"We wanted everything and got nothing," Klopp said, but the unspoken message to his players, the fans, and the world was clear: Liverpool would be back. For Klopp and Liverpool, the road to redemption had already begun.

# CHAPTER 12: THE MIRACLE UNFOLDS

The stage was set at Anfield for what would become one of the most iconic and memorable European nights in Liverpool's storied history. It was a night that would defy belief. Facing a seemingly insurmountable three-goal deficit from their previous encounter with Barcelona at Camp Nou, Liverpool prepared themselves for an epic showdown in the 2018/19 Champions League semi-final second leg.

## Confronting the Unthinkable

Klopp, always candid and forthright, couldn't deny the massive challenge they faced. He acknowledged, "Beating Barcelona is one of the toughest tasks in football; doing it when you're 3-0 down makes it even harder." The odds were firmly stacked against them, but Klopp's Liverpool had something intangible that would prove to be their greatest asset – an unwavering belief.

## Forging a New Legacy

Klopp had always emphasised the importance of creating their own history, stating, "We want to create our own history – not because we aren't proud of the club's history, but because we need new chapters." And on that unforgettable night at Anfield, his players wrote a new chapter into the annals of Liverpool's European adventures.

The match itself was an emotional rollercoaster. Liverpool knew they needed goals, and they delivered them with flair and audacity. Klopp couldn't help but marvel at the sheer brilliance of Trent Alexander-Arnold's corner kick that led to the fourth goal, labelling it as "sheer genius." This moment wasn't just a testament to individual skill but showcased the inventive spirit that Klopp had instilled in his Liverpool side.

Klopp reflected, "This club is a blend of atmosphere, emotion, desire, and football quality." Anfield, pulsating with fervour, played a pivotal role in the historic comeback, as the fans roared their team on against all odds.

## Against All Odds

Klopp had instilled massive belief in his players, even when the odds seemed fully stacked. He revealed, "How can you be sure before a game? I told the boys, 'I think it's impossible, but because it's you, we have a chance.' And we believed in that chance." This unwavering faith propelled Liverpool to a victory that would reverberate through the footballing world.

With the triumph over Barcelona, Liverpool found themselves within touching distance of Champions League glory. Klopp eagerly looked ahead to the final, declaring, "We're heading there in three weeks – it's like a pre-season for us, and I'm excited about it." The dream of lifting the coveted trophy was within grasp, and Klopp was determined to seize it.

In the aftermath of the historic win, Klopp couldn't contain his emotions, stating, "This club touches you deeply; you feel it more than others in moments like these. It's incredible, and I cherish it." It was a profound and unbreakable connection between a manager, his team, and the fans, creating a night that would forever be etched in their hearts and minds.

As Liverpool's remarkable journey in the Champions League continued, the world bore witness to a footballing miracle. Jurgen Klopp hadn't just revitalised a football club; he had reignited the magic of European nights at Anfield, reminding the world why Liverpool FC was truly exceptional.

# CHAPTER 13: MADRID TRIUMPH AND PREMIER LEAGUE TRIALS

The 2018-2019 Premier League season would be etched in footballing memory as one of the most thrilling and emotionally charged campaigns for Liverpool. It was a season marked by monumental highs and heart-wrenching lows, where the pursuit of Premier League glory took centre stage.

## The Catalyst in Goal: Alisson's Impact

The football community buzzed with animated discussions as Klopp secured the services of Brazilian goalkeeper Alisson Becker from AS Roma for a staggering £67 million—a world record fee for a goalkeeper. This was not just a transfer; it was a statement of intent.

Addressing the Elephant in the Room

Klopp had previously expressed concerns about the spiralling costs in football transfers, famously commenting on the exorbitant spending some clubs indulge in. Yet, here he was, sanctioning a massive fee for a goalkeeper. Klopp addressed this apparent contradiction head-on.

The Changing Landscape of Football Finance

"In football, sometimes, the landscape changes in the blink of an eye," Klopp might have noted. "A couple of years back, £100 million was a ludicrous figure. But now, that's just the way the game has evolved. It's a new reality."

"I'll do whatever it takes to make Liverpool successful," Klopp explained.

Liverpool's Transfer Strategy

While Alisson's signing captured headlines, it was part of a broader strategy. Naby Keita, Fabinho, and Xherdan Shaqiri were also recruited, strengthening the team and signalling Liverpool's ambitions.

Then there was the signing of Virgil van Dijk for £75 million. It was a move that had many second-guessing, but the towering defender soon proved his worth, becoming an important leader on the pitch.

Early Intent

The season commenced with Liverpool displaying their intent, winning their opening seven league games. The attacking trio of Mohamed Salah, Sadio Mane, and Roberto Firmino was firing on all cylinders, striking fear into opposing defences. Liverpool wasn't just winning; they were playing football that was not only effective but also exhilarating to watch.

Liverpool's Derby Delight

Anfield, December 2nd, 2018: Klopp's Liverpool carved out a dramatic 1-0 victory over Everton in the Merseyside Derby, a win that was as much about tactics and perseverance as it was about a slice of luck in the 96th minute.

Klopp, in a post-match press conference, shared his insights on the match that kept Liverpool in hot pursuit of Manchester City at the top of the Premier League table. The game's climax arrived deep in stoppage time. Substitute Divock Origi capitalised on an error from Everton goalkeeper Jordan Pickford to score a remarkable goal. Klopp, expressing his emotions about the winner, said, "Of course, it was a bit lucky - Virg, in the moment when the ball left his foot I thought it was over." He acknowledged the role of fortune as the ball hit the crossbar, leading to an "unthankful job for Pickford" and setting the stage for Origi's decisive header.

He described the match as a 'proper fight, a proper derby' characterised by high pressing and counter-pressing at the highest level. "Both teams delivered a proper fight, a proper derby from the first second," he remarked, emphasising the intense nature of the contest. The gaffer didn't miss the chance to praise Everton's performance, led by Marco Silva. "I told him how much I respect his work because it is incredible what he has done with that team. They are just an outstanding side," he stated, highlighting the challenges posed by the Toffees.

Klopp's strategic masterclass was evident in Liverpool's control of the game. Despite Everton's tight spaces, Liverpool managed to create moments of threat. "Our high-pressing was outstanding, our counter-press was really at the highest level, football-wise in a lot of moments it was really good," Klopp observed, praising the team's overall performance.

He also touched upon Divock Origi's journey, especially his recovery from a significant injury sustained in a previous derby. "I had it in my mind and never forgot it... he was an unbelievable threat: speed, physically strong. So it was always in my mind when I thought about Div," Klopp reflected, marking this goal as a significant moment in Origi's career.

Klopp lauded Fabinho's individual performance.

"He did a few outstanding one-on-one situations," Klopp noted, highlighting the midfielder's ability to handle pressure in critical moments of the game.

The victory was crucial for Liverpool's title aspirations, as evident in Klopp's strategic substitutions of Salah and Firmino. Looking forward, he hinted at potential rotations in the squad, considering the intense schedule ahead. "We only have to think about Burnley, not Bournemouth or Naples or [Manchester] United or Wolves," he concluded, focusing on the immediate challenges.

## The Battle with Manchester City

As the season progressed, the battle for the Premier League title intensified. Liverpool and Manchester City were locked in a relentless pursuit of each other. The two teams were setting a blistering pace, trading blows with every matchday.

A crucial clash with Manchester City at the Etihad Stadium was a pivotal moment in the title race. Liverpool went toe-to-toe with the reigning champions but narrowly lost 2-1. It was a bitter pill to swallow, as the margin for error had become razor-thin.

The Final Push

Liverpool's resilience shone through in the face of adversity. They embarked on a stunning run of victories, rekindling hopes of a long-awaited Premier League title. Late winners and remarkable comebacks became the norm, with the team showing unwavering determination.

One of the standout moments was the 3-2 victory over Newcastle United. Liverpool came from behind to secure a crucial win, with Origi once again delivering a late winner. The sense of destiny was palpable, and the fans dared to dream.

As the season entered its final stretch, Liverpool found themselves neck and neck with City. Every match was a must-win, and the pressure was immense. Liverpool's 4-0 victory over Huddersfield Town was a masterclass in keeping their title hopes alive, but fate had one final twist.

Missing Out on the Premier League Title

Liverpool's 2018/19 Premier League campaign was nothing short of remarkable. Klopp's Reds had displayed relentless determination, skill, and teamwork throughout the season. However, despite their impressive efforts, they fell agonisingly short of clinching the title.

On the final day of the season, Liverpool faced Wolverhampton Wanderers at Anfield. The team did their part, securing a comfortable 2-0 victory. Sadio Mane's goals had momentarily lifted the spirits of Liverpool supporters, and for a brief period, they dared to dream.

For 21 minutes, Anfield was a cauldron of hope and anticipation as Liverpool took the top spot on the live league table. Celebrations erupted as news of Brighton's goal against Manchester City filtered through. The atmosphere was electric, but it was false hope.

As City roared back to secure a 4-1 victory against Brighton, the dream began to slip away. Klopp acknowledged the surreal atmosphere during those moments, with fans anxiously awaiting news from the Amex Stadium.

Klopp's Gracious Congratulations

Despite the heartbreak of narrowly missing out on the title, Klopp showed his sportsmanship by offering heartfelt congratulations to Manchester City. He recognized the excellence of City's season, where they amassed an incredible 98 points.

Klopp stated, "Congratulations to Manchester City. They had an incredible season. We did as well, but they won it. We had an unbelievable season. I can read all the numbers. It would be nice to get an award for the biggest development I can remember – we made a big step."

Klopp's words also revealed his unwavering determination. He knew that Liverpool had come tantalisingly close to the Premier League title but had fallen short. However, he made it clear that this setback wouldn't deter his team.

"But I am not worried that this is as good as it can be," Klopp asserted. "As long as Manchester City are around with their financial power, no team will pass them easily. We need to be very close to perfection to win the Premier League as long as this is the case. There is more to come from us. If we are ready to make the next step, we will. That is the plan."

Klopp's optimism about Liverpool's future was evident. He believed that the team could continue to grow and evolve. The disappointment of the near-miss would fuel their determination to strive for greatness.

As he put it, "We will go again but give me a few hours to get over that."

While the Premier League title had eluded them that season, Klopp and his team had left their mark on the footballing world. Their journey was far from over, and the pursuit of glory would continue in the Champions League final.

## Glory in Madrid

June 1, 2019, at the Wanda Metropolitano in Madrid, was a night etched in the memories of the Reds' faithful. It was the stage for the ultimate showdown of European club football, where Liverpool would face Tottenham Hotspur in an all-English UEFA Champions League final. The atmosphere was electric, and the stakes were sky-high. After narrowly missing out on the Premier League title to City, Liverpool's entire season hinged on this one final match.

This was Klopp's third major European final with Liverpool, and the question on everyone's lips was whether his tactical brilliance could finally deliver the prize that mattered the most.

The tactical battle between Klopp and his counterpart, Mauricio Pochettino, began from the opening moments. Both teams knew each other well, and Klopp was aware that to overcome Spurs, he needed to neutralise their dynamic attacking threats. The German tactician set up his team in a 4-3-3 formation, a structure he had relied on throughout the season, instilling discipline while encouraging the forwards to exploit spaces.

Liverpool's approach paid dividends almost instantly. Within the first minute, a quick move saw the ball touch the hand of a Tottenham player in the box, and the referee pointed to the spot. The decision was controversial, but Mohamed Salah stepped up. He thundered the ball into the net, sending Liverpool fans into a frenzy. This goal, just 1 minute and 48 seconds into the match, was one of the quickest ever scored in a Champions League final.

Tactical Tenacity

Following the goal, the game settled into a rhythm, with Tottenham trying to find a way through Liverpool's disciplined structure. Klopp's tactical astuteness was on display as he instructed his team to sit a bit deeper, absorb pressure, and rely on the counter. This cautious approach was a deviation from the high-intensity pressing his team was known for.

Liverpool's midfield trio, led by captain Jordan Henderson, worked tirelessly. They were the cogs in Klopp's machine, winning back possession and releasing the front three to capitalise on Spurs' high defensive line. This relentless midfield battle was key to blunting the creative forces of Spurs, who found themselves stifled time and again.

On the rare occasions that Tottenham did breach the midfield line, they found a red wall waiting. Virgil van Dijk, the towering centre-back, was imperious, reading the game with an almost clairvoyant precision. Joel Matip partnered seamlessly with Van Dijk, and together they repelled Spurs' forays forward. Full-backs Trent Alexander-Arnold and Andy Robertson provided both defensive solidity and attacking support, encapsulating the dual role Klopp demands of his wide defenders.

As the game wore on, Tottenham began to carve

out opportunities. It was here that Liverpool's number one, Alisson Becker, demonstrated why Klopp had invested heavily in him. His saves were not just reflexive shot-stopping but a testament to his positional awareness and composure under pressure. Alisson's performance was a keystone of Liverpool's strategy — his safe hands allowed Klopp's tactical setup to hold firm.

The Game-Changing Moment

Klopp's game plan was crystal clear: keep things tight at the back and seize the perfect opportunity when it arises. That opportunity knocked on the 87th-minute door.

Amid relentless pressure from Spurs, Liverpool finally cleared their lines. The ball found its way to Divock Origi on the left side of the Tottenham penalty area. Origi, with a quick touch to set himself up, unleashed a powerful low shot that nestled into the far corner of the net. With that strike, he etched his name into Liverpool's history.

This was no ordinary match; it was a scorching battle, with both English titans grappling not only with each other but also with the sweltering heat. Klopp knew that dealing with a three-week break without a game was a unique challenge. "Tonight it was a big challenge for both teams to deal with the three-week [break] because you never have a period with three weeks and no game," he remarked.

Klopp didn't hold back in praising his team's ability to score at crucial moments and hailed Alisson's heroic saves. It was a night filled with raw emotion and sheer satisfaction for Liverpool.

As the press conference continued, talk of the next year's final being in Istanbul surfaced. Klopp, always forward-thinking, asserted with unwavering determination, "I told UEFA already:

we will be there!" He understood the weight of history and the expectations that came with being Liverpool, but he wasn't one to shy away from challenges. He knew that repeating such an achievement wouldn't be a walk in the park.

A Team Effort Like No Other

Klopp embraced the idea of collective effort that had brought Liverpool to this pinnacle of glory. He willingly shouldered the responsibility, allowing his players the freedom to showcase their footballing talents. For him, it was about guiding and supporting his team to ensure they performed at their absolute best.

It was a season marked by triumph, resilience, and the power of teamwork. From the heartbreak of narrowly missing out on the Premier League title to the sheer joy of conquering Europe, it was a rollercoaster ride that Liverpool and its fans will never forget.

# CHAPTER 14: CHAMPIONS OF ENGLAND

## Staying Grounded in Early Dominance

The following season, Liverpool hit the ground running. By the end of October, they had already secured significant victories, like the close 2-1 win against Leicester City, with a last-minute penalty by James Milner.

### The Key Victories

Every match seemed like a final, but Liverpool rose to the challenge each time. The impressive 3-1 win over Manchester City in November left the fans dreaming, but Klopp was cautious, knowing the season had many more battles ahead. "It's not important because who wants to be first in November? You want to be first in May," he maintained.

December brought a packed schedule, but Liverpool navigated it with ease. They secured a

Boxing Day victory against Leicester City with an emphatic 4-0 win that sent a strong message to their title rivals. Despite this, Klopp's message was clear: "If it would be easy to win the amount of games we have done, then more teams would have done it. It's not easy."

## Kings of the World

Winning the FIFA Club World Cup wasn't just about lifting a trophy Liverpool had never won before—it was about making a statement. This victory in Qatar was a testament to the Reds' unwavering spirit. Sure, there were questions— about human rights, about tossing the League Cup aside, about the travel during a crammed December. But once the lads started singing 'Campione, campione... Ole, ole, ole' in the dressing room, it was clear—all of it was worth it.

Klopp's boys had done something exceptional. They clinched the continental treble—the Champions League, the European Super Cup, and now the Club World Cup. No English team had ever done that before. Klopp beamed with pride, saying, "I am so proud of these boys."

Adam Lallana captured the mood perfectly, calling it an addiction—once you get a taste of victory, you just want more. And Joe Gomez was quick to point out how this win, this label of 'world champions', was a powerful surge of positivity.

Liverpool came back from Qatar not just as world champions but also as Premier League frontrunners. They were still leading the pack, with a game in hand.

Interestingly, the trip may have been a blessing in disguise. Klopp used it as a sort of warm weather training camp, an opportunity to drill his players without the constant pressure of games. The added belief from this win was just the cherry on top.

After such a high, there was little time for the Reds to rest. With the League Cup set aside, the focus sharpened on the prize they craved the most —the Premier League. With Leicester, Wolves, and Sheffield United waiting to challenge them, the road wasn't going to be easy. But Klopp and his men were ready.

Young Harvey Elliott, fresh from being part of the best club team in the world, was looking at a future bright with promise. There were injuries in the squad, yes, but there was also hope—hope that the likes of Minamino and Elliott could step up.

January tested Liverpool's mettle. A 2-0 win against rivals Manchester United at Anfield was a defining moment. The team was displaying champion qualities, and Klopp's influence was unmistakable. "We want to write our own stories, we want to create our own history," he said, as

Liverpool continued to set the pace at the top.

February brought a shock as Liverpool's invincible aura was pierced by Watford in a 3-0 defeat. Klopp didn't panic; he viewed it as a lesson. "We've never estimated the situation wrongly, we never thought it's easy. But of course, sometimes a little knock is important," he admitted. It was a minor blip on an otherwise stellar campaign.

## On The Brink of Glory

March saw the pandemic bring football to a standstill. But once play resumed, Liverpool picked up where they left off. A 4-0 win against Crystal Palace put them on the cusp of history. Klopp's philosophy shone through even as they edged closer to the title. "What is 'inevitable'?" he questioned, keeping everyone's expectations in check.

The Final Countdown

June 25th, 2020, became the date etched in the hearts of every Liverpool supporter. Chelsea's victory over Manchester City meant Liverpool were mathematically champions. The vision Klopp had set out was now a stunning reality.

The Explosion of Joy

Klopp described the moment when Liverpool's Premier League victory was confirmed. He said, "When we counted down the last five seconds of the game, the ref counted down a little bit longer than us so we had to look at two or three more passes! Then it was pure... I cannot describe it." His description captured the intense excitement and anticipation that filled the room as they waited for the final whistle. When the moment finally arrived, it was an "explosion" of emotions.

Despite the jubilation, Klopp confessed to feeling a sense of emptiness immediately after the victory. He admitted, "Directly after it, I felt so empty inside – I cannot believe it." This paradoxical mix of joy and emptiness highlighted the enormity of the achievement and the weight of expectations that had been lifted off his shoulders.

He assured everyone that he would be fine and that they need not worry about his emotional state. He expressed his happiness and acknowledged that he had never dreamed of such a moment before last year. Reflecting on the progress made over the past few years, Klopp marvelled at the consistency his team had displayed. He marvelled, "What the boys have done in the last two-and-a-half years, the consistency they show is absolutely incredible and second to none."

Klopp revealed that the Liverpool team had gathered to watch the Chelsea vs. Manchester City game, knowing that their title hopes hung in the balance. He emphasised the importance of having everyone together, stating, "There was no alternative." The manager, with his wealth of experience, insisted that every player had to be present to witness the historic moment. He believed that those who watched the game alone would regret it for the rest of their lives.

Jürgen Klopp's message to Liverpool fans around the world was simple but powerful: "It is for you out there. It is really for you." He expressed his hope that the fans felt the magnitude of the achievement and the love and dedication that the players and staff had put into this season. Klopp acknowledged the club's rich history and the contributions of legends like Kenny Dalglish, Graeme Souness, and Steven Gerrard. He was particularly pleased to deliver the title to Gerrard, who had shouldered immense pressure during his time at the club.

The Significance of Ending the 30-Year Wait

Klopp reflected on the significance of ending Liverpool's 30-year wait for a league title. He acknowledged the monumental journey the club had undertaken since their last league win and thanked the entire staff for their contributions. He praised the organisational skills of Ray Haughan, the nutrition expertise of Mona Nemmer, the fitness training by Andreas Kornmayer, and the soul that Pep Lijnders had infused into the team's style of play.

Klopp also highlighted the role of Vitor Matos in developing young talents within the club, mentioning players like Neco Williams, Curtis Jones, Harvey Elliott, Leighton Clarkson, and Jake Cain. The manager expressed his joy in working with coaches like John Achterberg and Jack Robinson, emphasising the collaborative effort of the entire coaching staff.

## Champions At Last

The trophy lift against Chelsea in a thrilling 5-3 victory at Anfield was more than a match; it was a celebration of a season that would be told for generations. Klopp had led a team not only to a championship but through one of the most extraordinary periods in modern history.

Klopp and his men stood tall as Champions of England. The road to this title was long and challenging, but it was conquered with a remarkable 99 points, a record at that time.

The Overwhelming Emotions

Klopp's initial response when asked to sum up his emotions was a heartfelt admission of his inability to do so. He said, "No, unfortunately not because if I tried to start talking about it [how I feel] again I will start crying again, and that doesn't work really well!" Klopp's tears of joy were a testament to the profound significance of the moment. He expressed being "completely overwhelmed" and revealed a mix of emotions that ranged from relief to happiness and pride.

In his own words, Klopp shared his thoughts: "I am relieved, I am happy, I am proud. I couldn't be more proud of the boys." It was evident that the journey had been long and challenging, making the triumph even sweeter for the manager.

# CHAPTER 15: REINVENTING LIVERPOOL AGAIN

## 2020/21: An Injury-Hit Season

The 2020/21 season was a rollercoaster ride for Liverpool. Coming off the back of the historic Premier League title win in the previous campaign, expectations were sky-high. However, the season was marked by injury setbacks, challenging results, and a determined quest for redemption.

Klopp faced one of the most challenging seasons of his managerial career. The relentless schedule and an alarming number of injuries put the team's title defence in jeopardy.

The Season Opener: A Sign of Things to Come

Liverpool's 2020/21 Premier League campaign

began with a thrilling 4-3 victory over newly-promoted Leeds United. While the result was positive, it was a foreshadowing of the defensive frailties that would plague the team throughout the season.

One of the defining narratives of Liverpool's season was the alarming number of injuries suffered by key players. Virgil van Dijk, Joe Gomez, and Joel Matip, all crucial components of Liverpool's formidable defence, suffered season-ending injuries early in the campaign. Klopp faced a monumental challenge in reorganising his defence, relying on inexperienced youngsters and makeshift centre-back pairings.

To counter the defensive crisis, Klopp adapted tactically. He employed midfielders like Jordan Henderson and Fabinho as makeshift centre-backs, a move that allowed Liverpool to maintain a competitive edge. Klopp's willingness to innovate and adapt showcased his tactical acumen and determination to navigate the season's challenges.

Despite the adversity, Liverpool's season was not without its moments of brilliance and memorable matches. Let's take a closer look at some of the key results and fixtures:

Merseyside Derby Triumph

In the first Merseyside Derby of the season, Liverpool secured a vital 2-0 victory against

Everton. Klopp's side displayed resilience and determination, with goals from Sadio Mané and Thiago Alcântara. This win lifted spirits and demonstrated Liverpool's capacity to compete even with a depleted squad.

Anfield's Fortress Falls

One of the most shocking results of the season came when Burnley ended Liverpool's 68-game unbeaten run at Anfield. Klopp acknowledged the frustration, saying, "It's my fault; I take the blame." The defeat marked a low point in the campaign but also ignited the team's determination to bounce back.

Clashes with Manchester United

In a crucial clash against title rivals Manchester United, Klopp's Liverpool played out a goalless draw. While the result was not ideal, the match showcased the tactical battle between Klopp and Ole Gunnar Solskjær. Klopp's tactical prowess was evident as Liverpool controlled large portions of the game.

In the return fixture at Old Trafford, Liverpool secured a resounding 4-2 victory. Klopp's side displayed their attacking prowess, with goals from Diogo Jota and Roberto Firmino. The win served as a statement of intent and rekindled hopes of a top-four finish.

The climax of Liverpool's season came on the final

day, as they faced Crystal Palace. A 2-0 victory ensured their place in the top four and Champions League qualification. Klopp's management during a challenging season played a significant role in achieving this crucial objective.

Throughout the 2020/21 season, Klopp's ability to adapt to adversity, guide his team through injuries, and secure a top-four finish highlighted his managerial excellence. Klopp's leadership provided a sense of stability during turbulent times, earning the respect and admiration of players, fans, and pundits alike.

## 2021/22: The Highs and Lows of a Historic Season

Liverpool's 2021/22 season was a rollercoaster of emotions, marked by breathtaking football and heartbreaking near-misses.

### Domestic Bliss

Domestically, Liverpool shone brightly, clinching the FA Cup and Carabao Cup. Their brand of football was electrifying, a testament to Klopp's tactical genius and the players' dedication. They pushed in the Premier League, too, toe-to-toe with City, eventually falling short by just a whisper— one point.

### European Nights

In Europe, the Reds were formidable. Each Champions League night at Anfield was a spectacle, a display of Klopp's "heavy metal football" that fans had come to expect.

## The Climax in Paris

The Stade de France set the stage for a duel with Real Madrid—a repeat of the 2018 final, a chance for redemption. The narrative was rich, the anticipation palpable.

Vinicius Jr's solitary goal was the dagger that pierced through the heart of Liverpool's aspirations. Thibaut Courtois, in Madrid's goal, was a colossus, denying Liverpool again and again.

## The Resonance of Defeat

Even as Klopp acknowledged Madrid's victory, his belief in his squad never wavered. "The boys played an outstanding season," he declared. The defeats in the league and Europe were by the narrowest margins—tests of spirit, but not indicators of failure.

Klopp's forward-looking optimism was evident. "The difference between 2018 and now is that I see us coming again," he confidently asserted.

Klopp understood the need for reflection, for the team to absorb the lessons of the season. "After a night's sleep and maybe another talk or speech from me, the boys will realise how special it was what they did," he said, already turning pain into motivation.

## 2022/23: The Fragility of Momentum

The 2022/23 season had come to a close, and Liverpool fans found themselves in unfamiliar territory. A thrilling 4-4 draw against relegated Southampton marked the end of a season that was far from their usual high standards. For the first time since the 2015/16 season, Liverpool narrowly missed out on a top-four finish. It was a season filled with ups and downs, but one thing remained crystal clear - the fragility of momentum in football. Klopp emphasised, "Momentum is the most fragile flower on the planet."

Liverpool's relentless schedule was a testament to their ambition - competing in all four competitions simultaneously. But Klopp was quick to point out the challenges that came with such a demanding routine.

Embracing the Demands

The life of a football manager, especially one at a top club like Liverpool, was anything but ordinary. It involved constant travel, ever-changing surroundings, and the weight of expectations from fans around the world. Klopp embraced this demanding lifestyle because he knew it was part and parcel of being a contender at the highest level.

While Liverpool remained focused on their title

pursuit, there was criticism from rival managers. Mikel Arteta, the Arsenal boss, voiced his displeasure over the fixture list, particularly when Arsenal had to face tough opponents like Chelsea and Manchester United in quick succession. He didn't hold back, saying, "Thank you so much to the Premier League to do that."

## Klopp's Singular Focus

In contrast, Klopp maintained his unwavering focus on Liverpool's own journey. He downplayed the importance of fixating on other teams' challenges and instead emphasised the need to win an extraordinary number of matches to secure the title. Klopp acknowledged the intense competition between Liverpool and Arsenal over the past few seasons, recognizing that it had elevated the standards of the Premier League.

"I don't think it is a problem for a human being every three days to be focused on what you do," Klopp remarked.

As Liverpool looked to reinvent themselves and regain their place at the top, Klopp's words served as a reminder that in football, momentum could be elusive, but with the right mindset and determination, they could once again rise to the challenge. The 2022/23 season might have been a test of their resilience, but Liverpool remained a force to be reckoned with in the world of football.

# PART IV: THE MIND BEHIND THE MAESTRO

# CHAPTER 16: KLOPP'S PHILOSOPHY

Jürgen Klopp's footballing philosophy is often likened to "heavy metal" football due to its high intensity and unrelenting nature. He coined this phrase to emphasise his preference for an aggressive, passionate approach to the game. Unlike the orchestrated, precise style associated with Arsene Wenger's teams, Klopp's football is more like a loud, energetic concert. He thrives on the chaos and fervour of the game, believing that this intensity is what sets his teams apart.

On the pitch, defending against Klopp's teams can be a daunting task. Players who faced them often found themselves bewildered by the organised chaos that unfolded. Curtis Davies, after Hull City's 5-1 defeat at Anfield, attempted to explain what it felt like. He pointed out that Klopp's side played with a unique level of freedom and fluidity. While it might appear chaotic, it's far from undisciplined. Klopp's teams are organised in their approach, and it's this organised chaos that poses problems for opponents. The players interchange positions, play beautiful football, and execute intricate passing moves that can overwhelm the opposition.

But Klopp's philosophy goes beyond the tactics on the pitch. He places significant emphasis on team cohesion and unity. According to Pepijn Lijnders, Klopp's assistant, "Jurgen creates a family. We always say: 30 percent tactic, 70 percent teambuilding." Beyond the tactics and strategies, Klopp believes in fostering a strong sense of camaraderie among his players. He understands that a united team is more likely to overcome challenges and achieve success.

One of the defining characteristics of Klopp's Liverpool is their ability to score quick, successive goals, often in moments of chaos on the pitch. German football writer Uli Hesse suggests that this is a direct reflection of Klopp's philosophy. While other modern coaches prioritise control and possession, Klopp thrives when the game becomes unpredictable and emotional. He values passion and determination over rigid tactics. In these moments of chaos, Klopp's teams are at their best.

Klopp is acutely aware of the dangers of complacency. He knows that too much comfort can lead to a decline in performance. He once stated, "It doesn't make it any easier to run your heart out when you've just woken up in a five-star hotel. Too much comfort makes you comfortable." To ensure his players remain motivated and hungry, Klopp occasionally introduces unique pre-season experiences and challenges that push them out of their comfort zones.

Klopp encourages his players to celebrate goals passionately as a team. He admires the way Barcelona celebrates goals, not necessarily for their style of play, but for their sheer enthusiasm. He believes that this level of passion and celebration is essential in football. It's a reminder of the joy and emotion that the sport can bring, something he wants his players to experience constantly.

The bond between Klopp and his players is a key aspect of his coaching philosophy. This deep connection fosters trust, commitment, and a shared sense of purpose. Players who fully embrace his philosophy are those who completely commit to his intense style of play. This bond is so strong that departures can be emotional, as seen when players like Shinji Kagawa and Mario Götze left Klopp's teams.

Sadio Mane, a key player under Klopp, highlights the importance of intensity in playing his style of football. According to Mane, Klopp often motivates the team to be angry and focused before every game. This intensity allows them to compete at their highest level and win crucial battles on the pitch.

Klopp's footballing preferences lean toward what he calls "English" football. He appreciates the gritty, competitive side of the game, especially during challenging conditions like rainy days and heavy pitches.

Klopp acknowledges the influences that have shaped his coaching philosophy. One notable influence is Wolfgang Frank, a former Mainz boss who introduced the pressing and defending style of play. Frank's revolutionary approach had a significant impact on German football, and Klopp continues to draw inspiration from it.

# Wolfgang Frank - The Mentor Behind Klopp's Mastery

Every great story has an origin, and Jürgen Klopp's tale of football management is deeply rooted in his time at Mainz 05, under the wing of Wolfgang Frank. It was here that Klopp discovered a game-changing approach to football. Wolfgang Frank wasn't just a coach; he was a football thinker who had a profound impact on Klopp's entire football ethos. Klopp soaked up every lesson from Frank, later recalling, "He showed us it wasn't about running more or fighting more but about being smarter and better organised than your opponent."

Frank introduced a style that was both practical and strategic, combining tough Italian defence with energetic pressing. This wasn't just about players kicking a ball; it was chess on a pitch. Klopp learned to see football in a new light—a team game where planning and teamwork were key. "We started to create plans for how to play against better-equipped teams," Klopp said, showing his early grasp of tactical discipline.

## Learning from the Best

Wolfgang Frank admired the work of the legendary Arrigo Sacchi and his AC Milan team. He believed in Sacchi's compact style, and Klopp was his eager student. This was a major building block for Klopp, who began understanding the game's deeper layers. Klopp would later say, "The best thing about football is that it's not about playing nice, it's about getting results," echoing Frank's practical teaching.

When Klopp took his first steps into management, he

carried Frank's blueprint but added his own intense twist to it. Klopp's teams don't just press; they swarm like bees, with purpose and precision. He often says it's not just running that wins games, it's running with reason.

Frank may not have been in the spotlight, but his teachings are visible in some of modern football's most thrilling moments. Through Klopp's triumphs, Frank's ideas have received a global stage. Klopp's gratitude is evident when he shares, "Wolfgang Frank was the first to show me the tactical aspect of the game."

Klopp's lively personality on the sidelines is a facade that hides a calculating mind, honed by years studying under Frank. "It's about making the right move at the right moment," Klopp has often remarked, reflecting the lessons from his mentor.

Watching Klopp's Liverpool is like a live demonstration of Frank's tactical legacy. The pressing, the teamwork, the intelligence on the pitch—it's all Frank's philosophy seen through Klopp's execution. This dynamic has made Liverpool not just a team of players but a synchronised unit with a shared brain.

# CHAPTER 17: LEADERSHIP STYLE

For Klopp, leadership is built on wholehearted dedication. He lives and breathes for the team, the players, and the club. In his own words, "As a leader, I try everything to be as successful as possible. I live 100 per cent for the boys, the boys, what we do for the club. I think that's leadership in the first case." This profound dedication serves as the foundation of Klopp's leadership philosophy.

## Leading by Example

He emphasises the importance of being a role model for his team: "As a leader, you cannot be the last who comes in and the first who goes out; you don't always have to be the first coming in or the last going out, but you have to be an example." In his actions and decisions, Klopp exemplifies the values and work ethic he expects from his players.

## Confidence and Humility

Confidence is a cornerstone of Klopp's leadership style. He recognizes its significance as a leader: "We have enough confidence, and that's very important for a leader. If I would expect from myself that I know everything and I'm the best in everything, I couldn't have confidence. But I don't expect that." Klopp's self-assuredness allows him to empower those around him. His confidence isn't about being a know-it-all; it's about enabling others to grow: "My confidence is big enough that I can really let people grow next to me, it's no problem." In essence, Klopp's confidence becomes a catalyst for the development and success of his team.

## Building a Supportive Team

Klopp understands that leadership is a collaborative effort. He values the expertise of those who surround him: "I need experts around me. It's really very important that you are empathetic, that you try to understand the people around you, and that you give real support to the people around you. Then everybody can act." Klopp's emphasis on empathy and support underscores the idea that great leaders don't stand alone; they create an environment where individuals thrive and work together seamlessly.

## Admitting Limitations

Klopp readily acknowledges that no leader possesses all the answers: "That's what leadership is: have strong people around you with a better knowledge in different departments than yourself, don't act like you know everything, be ready to admit, 'I have no clue in the moment, give me a couple of minutes and then I will have a clue probably.'" This humility fosters an environment of openness and continuous learning. Klopp's willingness to admit when he doesn't have all the answers encourages his team to seek solutions collaboratively.

Klopp's leadership style isn't confined to a rigid philosophy or a set of rules. It's a way of life, a genuine reflection of who he is: "That's how I understand it but it's no real 'philosophy,' it's just my way of life."

Appreciating the Fanbase

Beyond his team, Klopp acknowledges the profound impact of Liverpool's global fanbase: "This club is so unbelievably big, it's incredible... I sometimes try to imagine how it is in all the living rooms all over the world; millions and millions of people when we are playing are completely concentrated on what we are doing." Klopp's awareness of the fans' dedication adds an extra layer to his leadership style. He understands that his role extends beyond the pitch, embracing the responsibility of delivering joy to supporters.

In a footballing world filled with various leadership styles, Klopp's stands out as a testament to the power of dedication, humility, and the genuine care he has for his team and the fans.

## What Players Have Said About Klopp

Sadio Mané - The Confidante

The bond between Jürgen Klopp and Sadio Mané was more than just player and manager; it was a relationship that nurtured Mané's personal growth. Mané thrived under Klopp's guidance, evolving into a world-class forward. His feelings reflect the personal touch Klopp adds to his coaching, "He is a bit of a funny guy, but at the same time, he is a serious guy. Usually when I am talking to him off the pitch it is about personal things. Things about lifestyle and life – and that is important to me. I think I have somebody I can confide in.." That mix of light-heartedness and seriousness defined their time together, culminating in numerous trophies, including the coveted Champions League and Premier League titles.

Roberto Firmino - The Complete Forward

For Roberto Firmino, Klopp's influence has been transformative. The Brazilian forward credits Klopp with his holistic development, remarking, "I improved a lot in every way: physically, tactically, mentally." Firmino embodies the relentless energy and tactical intelligence that Klopp's system demands, and his improvement under the German is a testament to the meticulous and nurturing approach of Klopp's philosophy.

Ilkay Gundogan - The Emergence

When Ilkay Gundogan arrived at Borussia Dortmund, he was a diamond in the rough. Under Klopp's stewardship, he polished his game to shine brightly. Reflecting on his growth, Gundogan admits, "I struggled during my first six months... But thanks to the help of... Jürgen and his staff, too, I managed to improve." His ascent was pivotal in Dortmund's success, including winning the Bundesliga title and reaching the Champions League final in 2013.

Virgil van Dijk - The Colossus

For Virgil van Dijk, Klopp has been a critical figure in his rise to becoming one of the world's premier defenders. Their connection echoes the harmony of high expectations and mutual respect. "I have a very similar connection with Jurgen Klopp at Liverpool as I had earlier with Ronald Koeman at Southampton. Like Koeman, Klopp knows exactly how to get the best out of me – by being critical. When the media are hyping me and being very positive, he will downplay the praise and all that —often with a wink. And when I was voted UEFA Player of the Year and had to go to the ceremony, Jürgen told all the lads that I was picking up the trophy on behalf of the entire team," says Van Dijk, highlighting Klopp's knack for keeping his players grounded and focused.

Ivan Perisic - The Revelation

Ivan Perisic may not have spent a lengthy period under Klopp, but the impact was enduring. Klopp instilled in him the essence of modern football, teaching Perisic the importance of defensive work from the attacking front, transforming his approach to the game. "I was not used to defending from the front. I didn't even know that it was a two-way game. Jurgen taught me modern football," he asserts, pinpointing the tactical acumen he gained from the charismatic coach.

Henrikh Mkhitaryan - The Psychological Build

Henrikh Mkhitaryan's gratitude towards Klopp is profound. Amidst a challenging adaptation to the Bundesliga, Klopp was there to lift his spirits and bolster his mindset. "I am thankful to Klopp. He worked on my personality and the psychological part. Klopp showed me the way. He supported me and told me I had to keep my head up because good things were coming," Mkhitaryan reflects, underscoring Klopp's role in shaping not just the player, but the man.

Pierre-Emerick Aubameyang - The Personality

Klopp didn't just develop Aubameyang's skills on the pitch; he fortified his mental resilience and self-belief. Aubameyang's respect for Klopp is immense, "He taught me how to have a strong personality," a trait that has become a hallmark of the Gabonese striker's illustrious career.

Philippe Coutinho - The Maestro's Growth

Philippe Coutinho's ascendancy to one of football's creative aces was catalysed by Klopp's guidance. His time at Liverpool under Klopp was marked by breathtaking goals and assists, with Coutinho remarking, "He's just a great coach, one of the best in the world." His development under Klopp is a testimony to the manager's ability to nurture flair and creativity.

Mario Götze - The Prodigy

Mario Götze was just a budding talent when Klopp harnessed his potential. Under Klopp's tutelage at Dortmund, Götze became a German wunderkind, "He taught me everything about professional football. At that time, I was just 17 and coming up from the youth team. He introduced me to everything. He let me play," says Götze, who played a crucial role in Dortmund's domestic success and their Champions League journey during Klopp's tenure.

It's a little-known fact that Klopp has a hair transplant! Götze bumped into Klopp one day in Dusseldorf. He recalled, ""I have never met a manager in football who was so naturally funny . I will never forget the time I ran into him in Dusseldorf during the summer. He was going to see the specialist there to have his hair transplant done. This became big news in Germany, but he was so funny about it. He was smiling, telling me all about it — how cool it was going to look and everything."

"And then as he was leaving, he just gave me a wink and he said, 'Mario, don't worry, I will save the phone number.'

'What do you mean?' Götze replied

'The doctor's number. I'll save it for you. In a few years, you might need it.'

Robert Lewandowski - The Striker Supreme

Robert Lewandowski's transformation into a world-class striker is heavily credited to Klopp's influence. "I'm delighted I was able to get to know such a coach and such a person as Jürgen because he's amazing – both as a coach and a person. I learned so much from him and that means a lot," Lewandowski recalls, his prolific scoring helping Dortmund to significant silverware and establishing himself as one of football's leading forwards.

Divock Origi - The Clutch Performer

Divock Origi has become synonymous with crucial goals in big moments for Liverpool. He attributes such success to the fusion of Klopp's tactical prowess, the club's culture, and the fans' passion, encapsulating the holistic approach Klopp brings to the team.

Marco Reus - The Homecoming Star

Marco Reus's decision to join Dortmund was heavily swayed by the presence of Klopp. Reus thrived under Klopp, his game reaching new heights as he became a key player for both Dortmund and Germany. His awe of Klopp's persona is palpable, "If Jürgen sits in front of you... it's really quite impressive."

Trent Alexander-Arnold - The Local Hero

Trent Alexander-Arnold's meteoric rise from the

Liverpool academy to becoming one of the best right-backs in the world is a credit to Klopp's faith in youth. His gratitude is evident, "Obviously without him who knows what would've happened. He's the one that's given me the most opportunities, more than I could even ask for."

Each chapter of Klopp's career is punctuated by the growth of players who not only improved on the pitch but also developed a profound respect for the man behind their evolution. Their testimonies speak volumes, not just of a manager who shaped their careers, but of a mentor who left an indelible mark on their lives.

# CHAPTER 18: FAMILY AND PERSONAL LIFE

While Klopp is renowned for his coaching prowess and leadership on the field, it's important to understand the man behind the manager. In this chapter, we explore how his family and personal life play a significant role in shaping his character and decisions.

## Birth of His Son

In the hustle of the late '80s, a young Klopp, with his life teetering between the carefree days of youth and the daunting precipice of fatherhood, faced a crossroads that would shape the very core of the man he was to become. Klopp recalled, "When I was 20, I experienced the moment that completely changed my life. I was still a kid myself, but I had also just become a father. It was not perfect timing, let's be honest. I was playing amateur football and going to university during the day. To pay for school, I was working in a warehouse where they stored movies for the cinema."

In an era where the word 'streaming' was more likely to be associated with a runny nose than watching films, Klopp was grappling with metal canisters hefty enough to make even the strongest of backs groan. "Lifting those canisters was a workout in itself," Klopp might joke, "better than any gym session." But beneath the humour was the reality of a gruelling schedule: from the warehouse at dawn to university lectures, then to the football pitch, and finally home—to the most important role of all, being a father.

Learning Life Outside the 90 Minutes

For Klopp, these years were less about mastering the 4-4-2 formation and more about learning the delicate art of balance and sacrifice. While friends revelled in the night's promise, Klopp was already playing the long game, his decisions a testament to a maturity. The joy of a pub night paled in comparison to the joy of his son's smile, a trade-off he'd make every single time without regret.

It was during these days of hustle and little sleep that Klopp came face-to-face with life's authentic difficulties, a far cry from the trials on the football field. "There's real worry, and then there's football worry," he'd later say, with the wisdom of someone who knew that some lessons could only be learned in the trenches of real life.

Years later, fans and critics alike would question how Klopp could keep his smile, even when the scoreboard didn't favour his side. But they didn't see the whole picture. That smile was birthed from a place of deep understanding—that football, as much as it was his world, wasn't the be all and end all.

When the stakes were highest, not on the pitch, but in the quiet of night with his son cradled in his arms, Klopp found a perspective that would define his approach to the game. "Football is not life or death," he'd often remind his players and anyone who'd listen. The beauty of the game, for Klopp, was in its power to inspire, to bring joy, especially to the young fans whose dreams were as vivid and wild as his own ones were.

## A Welcoming Home in Liverpool

"I never thought that we would find again a place where we would feel that welcome," Klopp reflected. These words shed light on the deep connection he and his family have developed with Liverpool. Klopp's journey at Anfield has been defined by a sense of belonging and warmth from the community.

Liverpool has become more than just a workplace for Klopp; it's a second home where he and his family have found genuine acceptance. Liverpool's warm hospitality has undoubtedly left a mark on Klopp.

## Ulla's Influence

It all began with an encounter at Munich's Oktoberfest in 2005, where Ulla, then a waitress, caught the eye of the future Liverpool manager. Klopp found more than just festive cheer in those lively tents; he found a partner who would become his rock in both life and his career. Ulla, with her experience as a social worker and her flair as a novelist, brought depth and compassion to Klopp's life. Their connection was instant and profound. So profound that within days, they were living together, and within two months, they became husband and wife. Their whirlwind romance is a testament to the adage that when you know, you truly know.

Both having sons from previous relationships, they blended their families with the ease that only true love can bring. Ulla's son, Dennis, and Klopp's son, Marc, became part of a new family unit, centred around support and understanding.

Ulla's humility and dedication to charity work earned her the affectionate moniker 'The First Lady of Bundesliga' back in Germany. But her impact wasn't confined to just one country; her generosity stretched as far as Kenya, where she spent time as a teacher and hospital worker. It's this spirit of giving that saw Ulla, during the lockdown, quietly handing out £1,000 in vouchers to supermarket workers. No fanfare, no cameras — just a genuine act of kindness from a woman who understands the value of community and hard work.

The Klopps' journey has been one of mutual support. Ulla has been by Jurgen's side through the peaks and valleys of his career, from Mainz to Dortmund and now Liverpool. As Klopp orchestrated Mainz's promotion to the Bundesliga and redefined Dortmund, Ulla was the constant in his life, the person he turned to in moments of doubt and celebration.

Jurgen once said, "We sat at the kitchen table and Ulla said, 'I can't see us leaving in 2024,'" revealing the pivotal role she played in his decision to extend his contract with Liverpool.

The couple's move to Formby, into Steven Gerrard's former home, paints a picture of a life that, while grand, remains rooted in simplicity. They don't seek the limelight.. They visit local spots without fuss, and Ulla's absence from social media breaks the cycle from many WAGs out there.

While Klopp may be the face we see on the sidelines, it's Ulla's influence that steers many of his life decisions. Her impact goes beyond the personal; it touches the professional realm, where her insights and perspectives have been invaluable to him. Her low-key, approachable demeanour belies the significant role she plays as his confidant and counsel.

As we look at Klopp's success, it's essential to recognize the foundation upon which it's built: his relationship with Ulla. "Why? Is now the question. Because Ulla wants to stay and as a good husband what are you doing when your wife wants to stay? You are staying," Klopp shared when discussing his contract renewal.

## Faith

In a world where footballers and managers are

often seen as icons, Klopp points to a figure beyond the stadium who holds the ultimate significance for him. "Jesus Christ is the most important person in history," says Klopp, setting the foundation of his life on a cornerstone that, for him, surpasses every trophy and title.

Klopp's approach to his belief is much like his approach to football—active, vocal, and full of passion. "To be a believer, but not to want to talk about it - I do not know how it would work!" he declares. Just as he encourages his players to communicate on the field, he believes in expressing his faith openly.

He understands the struggle of balancing Sunday matches with Sunday services from his teenage years. Yet, he believes there's more than enough time throughout the week to cultivate his relationship with his faith.

Despite the pressures of football, Klopp finds a reassuring solace in his belief. "When I look at me and my life - and I take time for that every day - then I feel I am in sensationally good hands." It's a feeling of security that he wishes others could also experience.

Klopp likens the sacrifice of Jesus to the ultimate triumph, one that overshadows even the greatest of football victories. "He took all the sins on himself and was nailed on a cross... this was the greatest act that has ever been achieved, because it changed everything." For Klopp, this act of love is the ultimate source of comfort and motivation.

# CHAPTER 19: KLOPP AND THE MEDIA

Klopp is known for his warm smile and the hearty chuckle that often accompanies his conversations with the media. "I could be sleeping, but I'm here talking to you!" Klopp remarks, emphasising his commitment to the media.

Klopp's accessibility to the media doesn't stop at exclusive interviews. There are camera crews, podcast recordings, and duties for the club's TV channel. Being the manager of Liverpool is a 24/7 job, and the fun never stops.

## Early Aspirations

Intriguingly, Jurgen Klopp once confessed, "If football hadn't worked out, I probably would have ended up being a sports reporter." This revelation shines a light on his early aspirations in journalism. Martin Quast, a close friend of Klopp and a German journalist, recalls Klopp's internship at SAT1, Germany's first privately-owned TV station, during his playing days at Mainz in the 1990s.

One of Klopp's notable experiences as a journalist was a feature on the Roschingers, the highly successful snowboarders from the Hesse region. He interviewed the sisters, added a voice-over, and even edited the feature himself. Quast recalls, "He was talented."

Fortunately, or perhaps unfortunately for journalism, Klopp's destiny led him to football management instead. But his brief stint in journalism reveals a deep-rooted respect for the industry.

## Football's New Look on TV

The 1990 World Cup was not just a victory for Germany but a turning point for how football was experienced at home. SAT1's innovative broadcast approach brought the stadium's atmosphere into living rooms, blending match action with personal stories and off-pitch drama.

Klopp, reflecting on his stint as a pundit during the 2006 World Cup, realised its impact on his public recognition: "It was quite successful, it was a wonderful tournament, everybody was there, the weather was brilliant...my face every second day on television. Nobody really knew me then.

Not a problem, but the problem then was when I came home I still lived like a person who nobody cares about. But when I was in the garden trying to water the flowers, buses passed my house...waving at me, so we had to change a few things and adapt to the new situation."

This era introduced a narrative-rich form of sports broadcasting that combined the tactical aspects of the game with the emotional and personal elements, turning every match into a drama. Klopp's foray into punditry began notably at the Confederations Cup of 2005, where his expertise and candidness on ZDF wowed German viewers.

Winning Over British Viewers

In September 2016, Jürgen Klopp made a memorable appearance on Monday Night Football, a British football show, that would solidify his status not just as a top football manager but also as a media darling in the UK. As Liverpool's manager, he charmed viewers with a blend of candid insight and wry humour that had become his trademark.

Klopp looked back on his transition from player to manager, his self-deprecation and openness on full display. "One of my best things I did in my managing career was my first decision when I became a manager. I was a player the day before. And the first thing I said: 'But then I don't play anymore.' That helped the team a lot!"

Klopp's blend of strategic excellence and personal charisma won hearts, making his TV appearances as eagerly anticipated as Liverpool's matches. As he humorously dismissed the betting odds and discussed his frugal nature, "I don't even understand the numbers. Where I'm from, you keep your money."

## Complex Relationship

Klopp's interactions with the media are a blend of straightforwardness, professionalism, and a unique brand of humour. He is known for his candidness and directness, which sometimes leads to unconventional responses in press conferences. Klopp himself has stated, "Regarding the public, I'm super lucky because I really don't care at all what they think... Some might think 'there's a real nice bloke always in a good mood' and the others might say 'that smug git has been getting on my bloody tits for years'. But I don't have to worry about one or the other". This attitude exemplifies his disregard for public perception, focusing instead on what matters to him professionally and personally.

Klopp's professional approach to media interactions has been noted by Thomas Hennecke, an expert on Borussia Dortmund, who described Klopp's relationship with the media as "unbelievably professional" but also "downright direct". Klopp is known to take journalists to task personally if he feels misquoted or disagrees with a story, yet he doesn't hold grudges. This trait of confronting issues head-on and then moving on is admired by many journalists, as it provides clarity and transparency in interactions.

However, Klopp's directness can sometimes come across as short-tempered, especially when he's asked repetitive questions. Hennecke recalls a press conference where Klopp, frustrated by a repetitive question, asked the journalist if he'd been living in a cave for the past couple of months . This response, while humorous, also highlights Klopp's impatience with what he perceives as unnecessary or redundant media probing.

Klopp's media persona has been crucial in shaping the brand image of the teams he has managed.

His straightforward, honest approach resonates well with the mentality of places like the Ruhr region, where he managed Borussia Dortmund. His style, characterised by a mix of a big mouth, metaphorical language, and an easy-to-understand delivery, made him a media favourite.

Despite his forthrightness, Klopp also understands the power of media perception. He ended his activity as a TV football expert when he took over at Dortmund in 2008, fearing that his image as a media personality might overshadow his coaching role. This decision reflects his awareness of the importance of media perception in shaping a professional image.

Klopp's natural charisma and knack for catchy soundbites have made him popular with the media and fans alike. His spontaneous and jovial manner, especially in contrast to more reserved figures in football, has endeared him to many. For instance, his humorous quotes and engaging interviews have often been highlighted in the media.

However, Klopp's media relations have not always been smooth. There have been instances where he has openly expressed disappointment or frustration. For example, after a poor performance by his team, Klopp did not shy away from acknowledging their shortcomings in the media, reflecting his commitment to honesty and transparency.

# His Funniest Press Conference Moments

I've heard my fair share of managers' quips, but none are quite as entertaining as Klopp's. So, pull up a chair, and let's dive into the top ten funniest quotes that capture Klopp's infectious spirit.

### The Normal One

Right from his first day at Liverpool, Klopp made it clear he wasn't here to follow the usual script. When asked if he was the 'Special One' like José Mourinho, Klopp humbly and humorously positioned himself as 'The Normal One'. He quipped, "I am a normal guy from the Black Forest. I was a very average player. I don't compare myself with these genius managers from the past." With this one-liner, Klopp didn't just endear himself to fans; he also set the tone for his down-to-earth and relatable persona.

### A Player of Two Minds

Reflecting on his own playing career, Klopp once delivered a self-deprecating gem: "I never succeeded in bringing to the field what was going on in my brain. I had the talent for the fifth division, and the mind for the Bundesliga. The result was a career in the second division."

### David vs. Goliath: The Football Version

Klopp's tenure at Dortmund saw them constantly pitted against the Goliath of German football,

Bayern Munich. His underdog mentality was perfectly captured when he said, "We have a bow and arrow and if we aim well, we can hit the target. The problem is that Bayern has a bazooka. The probability that they will hit the target is clearly higher. But then Robin Hood was apparently quite successful."

### Celebrating an Epochal Victory

When Dortmund conquered the Allianz Arena after a long drought, Klopp's remark was both poignant and hilarious: "When Dortmund last won here 19 years ago, most of my players were still being breast-fed." It's vintage Klopp.

### Sarcasm and Transfers

The transfer saga of Mario Götze to Bayern made headlines, and Klopp's reaction was laced with his characteristic sarcastic wit: "He's leaving because he's Guardiola's favourite. If it's anyone's fault, it's mine. I can't make myself shorter and learn Spanish."

### The Broomstick Promise

Klopp has always been vehemently against unfounded transfer rumours. When Mats Hummels was linked with Manchester United, Klopp retorted, "If that's not a bull**** story, I'll eat a broomstick!"

### A Good Wife's Patience

The loyalty and patience Klopp shows his players

were beautifully expressed when he likened waiting for Hummels' return from injury to, "a good wife waiting for her husband who is in jail."

Casualties of Celebration

Celebrations can sometimes lead to mishaps, and Klopp knows this all too well. After a wild victory celebration where Klopp broke his glasses, he remarked, "One [pair] is in the museum of Borussia Dortmund because we won for the first time against Bayern Munich and Nuri Sahin broke my first glasses. Today it was Adam, it's broken."

The Forgotten Legend

When speaking of Genk's academy and its famous graduates, Klopp interrupted a journalist to remind him of Divock Origi, saying, "Don't forget that. Liverpool legend, by the way. Pretty famous here." Origi's crucial goals for Liverpool had etched him in the club's folklore, and Klopp didn't miss the chance to cheekily remind everyone of his heroics.

Explaining the Inexplicable

Finally, Klopp's sharp wit was on display when a Schalke fan inquired about the secret to winning titles. Klopp's response? "How do you explain to a blind person what colour is?"

Cheers, Jürgen, for keeping the fun in football!

# PART V: LEGACY AND INFLUENCE

# CHAPTER 20: KLOPP'S IMPACT ON GERMAN FOOTBALL

## The Blend of Styles: Vertical Tiki-Taka

Klopp's approach to football wasn't limited to just Gegenpressing. He ingeniously blended elements of traditional "Tiki-Taka" with a direct, vertical style. This fusion of tactics created a unique brand of football that entertained fans and bewildered opponents.

His teams played with quick transitions, sharp passing, and a relentless attacking mentality. This style was particularly effective against teams that employed a more possession-based approach. Klopp's ability to adapt and merge these different philosophies showcased his tactical acumen and made football accessible and exciting for the average fan.

Pressing from the Front

Klopp's philosophy emphasised pressing from the front, disrupting the opponent's build-up play before it could even begin. This high-pressure approach redefined defensive strategies in German football and set a benchmark for intensity and organisation.

## Development of Young Talent

Beyond tactical innovations, Klopp's influence extended to player development. He had an eye for talent and a knack for nurturing emerging stars. His trust in young players like Mario Gotze, Mats Hummels, and Robert Lewandowski paid dividends for both the players and their clubs.

Klopp's mentorship played a pivotal role in

shaping these talents into world-class footballers. Their successes served as a testament to his ability to identify and harness potential, and it gave hope to young footballers dreaming of making it big.

Klopp's commitment to promoting homegrown talents was evident throughout his managerial career in Germany. He believed in giving youth academy graduates a chance to shine on the big stage. This approach not only benefited the players but also inspired other Bundesliga clubs to invest in their academies and provide opportunities for local talents.

His emphasis on nurturing local talent created a pathway for young footballers to dream of representing their hometown clubs, further strengthening the bond between clubs and their communities. It was a nod to the grassroots.

## Influence on Future Managers

Klopp, throughout his career, has demonstrated a unique knack for being the underdog and using it to his advantage. As former Dortmund boss Thomas Tuchel aptly put it, "Klopp is the master of being the underdog." Tuchel, who faced Klopp's Liverpool side in the FA Cup Final, acknowledged Klopp's uncanny ability to frame his team as underdogs even when facing formidable opponents like Villarreal and Benfica in the Champions League.

Tuchel's words shed light on how Klopp's influence extended beyond the touchline and into the hearts of football enthusiasts. Klopp had the power to convince, to make people believe that his team could overcome the odds, and he did it with a sense of humour and charm that few could resist.

# CHAPTER 21: GLOBAL INFLUENCE

## Common Goal Charity

Klopp's influence extends far beyond the football pitch. He's not just an exceptional coach but also a compassionate human being who utilises his platform to make a difference in the world.

In September 2019, Klopp joined forces with the Common Goal charity, a pledge-based initiative within the football industry. He revealed this commitment while accepting the Men's Coach of the Year prize at the Best FIFA Football Awards. Klopp, whose annual earnings as Liverpool's manager amount to approximately £10 million, pledged to donate 1% of his salary to various football-related charities worldwide. This substantial contribution underscores his unwavering dedication to using football as a catalyst for positive change.

Klopp stated, "I want to be part of a movement that is supporting the great work football is doing around the world. Common Goal is a simple and effective way for the football community to give back." His decision to contribute a percentage of his significant earnings to charitable causes demonstrates his commitment to making a meaningful impact through football.

Supporting South African Children's Football Charity: Empowering Young Hearts

In October 2019, Klopp demonstrated his generosity by contributing £10,000 (approximately 235,000 Rands) to the Joy is Round initiative, managed by Hout Bay United Football Community in South Africa. This charity's mission is to promote and fundraise for the development of football within South African communities. Klopp's support reflects his commitment to empowering young football enthusiasts across the globe.

Klopp's contribution to the Joy is Round initiative underscores his dedication to improving the lives of young individuals through football. His willingness to support grassroots initiatives in South Africa highlights the global impact of his philanthropic efforts.

Sean Cox Fundraiser: Standing in Solidarity

He contributed around £4,400 (€5,000) to the

Sean Cox fundraiser. This initiative was launched to assist Sean Cox, an Irish Liverpool fan who was brutally attacked by AS Roma fans before a Champions League match. The funds raised were intended to aid Cox's recovery and cover medical expenses.

Klopp expressed his support, saying, "Sean's story has touched all of us, and it's clear that his family and loved ones are not walking this path alone. We are in this together."

Prostate Cancer Aid Fundraiser: Prioritising Human Health

Jurgen Klopp acknowledges the paramount importance of health and well-being. He made a substantial donation of £4,000 to the Michael Edwards' Men in Lycra Just Giving Page, which supported the aid of Prostate Cancer in the UK. Through gift aid, Klopp's contribution reached £5,000, helping the page swiftly reach its fundraising target. His involvement in this fundraiser underscores his commitment to supporting causes related to human health and well-being.

Klopp emphasised, "The health of human beings is the most important thing in the world. Let's stand together and make a difference." His contribution to the Prostate Cancer Aid Fundraiser reflects his dedication to improving the well-being of individuals, even beyond the football field.

Participation in a Charity Match:
Uniting for a Noble Cause

In 2018, Klopp participated in James Milner's charity match, titled 'a match for cancer.' This friendly match, co-sponsored by the James Milner Foundation, featured renowned football players such as Dirk Kuyt, Robbie Keane, and Luis Garcia. The event aimed to raise funds to combat cancer in the UK.

Klopp reflected, "Football has the power to unite people and make a positive impact on society. I'm honoured to be part of this charity match." His participation in such events showcases his commitment to using football as a platform for social change and the betterment of society.

## Educational Initiatives and Mentorship

Klopp's willingness to mentor young coaches and share his insights has contributed to his global influence. He actively participates in coaching seminars, educational programs, and mentorship relationships, passing on his knowledge to the next generation of football leaders.

Klopp's emphasis on youth development and providing young players with opportunities has resonated with football academies worldwide. Clubs are increasingly implementing similar strategies, promoting youth talent and creating pathways to the first team.

Klopp's success in developing talents like Trent Alexander-Arnold and Curtis Jones has set a benchmark for youth development programs. Young coaches recognize the importance of nurturing and developing young talents, and Klopp's achievements serve as a reminder of the potential within youth academies.

Building Bridges Through Football

Jurgen Klopp's international appeal has helped bridge cultural divides through football. His presence has fostered connections between Liverpool FC and fans from diverse backgrounds and nations. Klopp's message of unity and inclusivity aligns with football's power to bring people together, transcending borders and languages.

Klopp's ability to connect with fans worldwide showcases football's ability to transcend cultural and linguistic barriers. His impact extends beyond the pitch, reminding coaches and players of the global reach of the sport they love.

Klopp's ability to connect with fans from different backgrounds and cultures has helped build bridges through the sport of football, promoting unity and inclusivity.

Klopp's legacy serves as a reminder of the impact one individual can have in the world of football and beyond. His commitment to philanthropy, mentorship, and promoting positive values will continue to inspire generations to come.

# CHAPTER 22: THE KLOPP EFFECT ON LIVERPOOL

Klopp's tenure as Liverpool manager has been nothing short of transformative. Beyond the silverware and on-field success, his influence has left an indelible mark on the club. In this chapter, we delve into the enduring legacy of Klopp's impact on Liverpool, examining how he has shaped the club's playing style, infrastructure, youth development, and community engagement.

## Anfield Expansion: A Symbol of Ambition

The Anfield Road End expansion is a project close to Jürgen Klopp's heart, underlining Liverpool FC's future-focused ambition. Klopp's words show the ambition of the club, "It's incredible. It's going to be a special place to play. The atmosphere at Anfield is already amazing, and this is just going to make it even better," he remarked, picturing the buzz that an additional 7,000 fans will bring.

Klopp, in characteristic fashion, infused his enthusiasm into the ceremonial commencement of the expansion. Despite a delay owing to the pandemic, he was at the forefront, symbolically initiating this massive undertaking. His eagerness is evident as he looks forward to the completion of the expansion, "I really hope they will finish it in time... It's a sign that we're moving in the right direction," Klopp asserts. He sees the expansion as a pillar of the club's strategy to grow and sustain its competitive edge.

Mental Strength: A Key Ingredient

In addition to honing technical skills, Klopp places a strong emphasis on mental strength. He understands that successful footballers need to be mentally resilient to cope with the pressures of the game. Klopp states, "You have to be mentally strong to be a successful footballer. You have to be able to deal with pressure and setbacks."

Klopp's focus on mental resilience has been evident in Liverpool's ability to mount comebacks and handle high-stakes situations. The "never give up" mentality instilled by Klopp has become a hallmark of Liverpool's playing style.

# Youth Development: A Priority

Klopp prioritises youth development during his tenure at Liverpool. He firmly believes in providing opportunities to young talents and emphasises that "I don't think it's possible to bring a local player through just because he's a local player. But first of all, we have to learn that we have to give these young players a chance."

Klopp advocates for creating an environment where young players can learn and develop, stating, "Give them the opportunity to play first-team football." He recognizes the importance of patience in the development process, emphasising, "We have to be patient. It takes time to develop young players."

Under Klopp's guidance, Liverpool has seen the emergence of young talents like Trent Alexander-Arnold and Curtis Jones. Klopp's commitment to nurturing the next generation of football stars aligns with Liverpool's historical focus on producing top-quality players from its youth academy.

Holistic Approach: Beyond the Pitch

Jurgen Klopp's impact on Liverpool extends far beyond the confines of the football pitch. His commitment to community engagement and social initiatives exemplifies a holistic approach to football.

Klopp actively participates in charitable

endeavours and fundraisers, demonstrating his dedication to making a positive impact on society. His involvement in various initiatives showcases his desire to use his platform as Liverpool manager to contribute to the greater good.

Klopp's legacy at Liverpool represents more than just football success. It embodies a philosophy, a vision, and a commitment to the club's future. His influence is felt in every aspect of Liverpool's operations, from how they play on the pitch to how they engage with the community.

# CHAPTER 23: WHAT'S NEXT FOR KLOPP?

Jurgen Klopp's remarkable journey with Liverpool has been a rollercoaster ride of success and transformation. Fans are eager to know what the future holds for this iconic manager. While Klopp has been relatively tight-lipped about his specific plans, there are several intriguing possibilities to consider when speculating on what's next for him.

## Contract Expiry and Potential Extension

Klopp's current contract with Liverpool is set to expire in 2026. Klopp himself has previously stated that he intends to take a break from coaching when his Liverpool contract comes to an end. In his own words, "I will take a one-year break after Liverpool." However, he has also made it clear that he loves coaching and has no intention of retiring from the game in the near future. So, while a sabbatical may be on the horizon, don't count out the possibility of Klopp extending his stay at Liverpool or taking on a new challenge.

## International Management

One intriguing path for Klopp's future is international management. Klopp has expressed a genuine interest in coaching a national team at some point in his illustrious career. Given his deep ties to the German national team, having managed Borussia Dortmund and boasting an impressive coaching resume, the allure of leading Germany could be enticing. Klopp acknowledges the honour of managing one's country's national team, saying, "It is a great honour to manage your country's national team." With the possibility of a vacancy arising after the 2026 World Cup, it's a prospect that could become a reality.

## Academic Pursuits: A Thoughtful Intellectual

Klopp is not just a football manager; he's also a thoughtful intellectual with a degree in sports science. He has occasionally delved into discussing the psychological aspects of the game and tactics. It wouldn't be surprising to see Klopp involved in academic or analytical aspects of football in the future. Perhaps he will contribute to sports science research, write books about his coaching philosophy, or share his insights in educational programs. Klopp's passion for the game and his intellectual curiosity make him a natural candidate for such endeavours.

## Community and Charitable Work

Klopp's commitment to community engagement and charitable initiatives is well-known. Regardless of his future in football management, he is likely to continue making a positive impact on society through philanthropic efforts. His involvement in social causes and charity work is a testament to his character and his desire to give back to the community.

## Continuing the Klopp Legacy

Whoever succeeds Jurgen Klopp at Liverpool faces the daunting task of following in his footsteps. Klopp's influence on the club is profound, and his successor will need to carry forward his philosophy while making their mark. Klopp himself will undoubtedly keep a close eye on Liverpool's progress and may remain connected to the club in some capacity. His love for Liverpool fans and the incredible atmosphere they create at Anfield is well-documented. Klopp once said, "The most boisterous fans in the German top flight are Borussia Dortmund supporters, but Liverpool fans are even more extreme." He finds the passion of Liverpool fans to be unmatched and has referred to it as "insane." Klopp's presence and support will likely continue to resonate at Anfield, even if he's not in the manager's dugout.

The future for Jurgen Klopp is uncertain, but it's filled with intriguing possibilities. While he has been cautious not to reveal too much about his plans, his love for the game, passion for coaching, and desire to make a positive impact on and off the pitch suggest that he will remain a prominent figure in the football world, wherever his journey takes him. Klopp's legacy at Liverpool and his influence on the sport as a whole will undoubtedly endure for years to come, making him one of the most beloved and respected figures in football history.

# CHAPTER 24: FINAL THOUGHTS

Jurgen Klopp's journey through the world of football has been nothing short of extraordinary. From his earliest days on the pitch to his transformative managerial career, one thing has remained constant: his unwavering passion for the beautiful game. Football is more than just a profession for Klopp; it's a lifelong love affair.

Klopp's infatuation with football began at an early age. Growing up in the small town of Glatten, Germany, he was drawn to the sport like a moth to a flame. The local pitch was his playground, where he honed his skills and developed a deep connection with the game. His childhood dreams were filled with images of goals scored, victories celebrated, and the roar of the crowd.

"Life is too short not to celebrate nice moments!" Klopp once exclaimed, and his career has been filled with plenty of such moments. He understands the importance of cherishing the journey and finding joy in every success, no matter how big or small.

Before he became known as "The Normal One" or "Kloppo," Jurgen Klopp was simply a footballer with dreams of making it big. While his playing career may not have reached the illustrious heights of his managerial success, it provided him with invaluable experiences that would shape his understanding of the sport.

"Anyone can have a good day, but you have to be able to perform on a bad day," Klopp mused, reflecting on the ups and downs of his playing days. He learned the importance of resilience and determination, qualities that would serve him well in his future role as a manager.

## The Klopp Way

He believes in the power of "Total Football," a concept where every player on the pitch is expected to contribute both defensively and offensively.

"In the Premier League, there's five, six, or seven clubs that can be the champions," Klopp acknowledged. The competition is fierce, and success is hard-fought. Klopp's coaching philosophy is built on the recognition that achieving greatness requires not only skill but also resilience and consistency.

For Klopp, a player's first touch is sacrosanct: "The first touch is the most important thing in football. If you can control the ball well, then you have time to think and make the right decision." He further emphasised the central role of passing in football: "If you want special results, you have to feel special things and do special things together."

But Klopp's philosophy isn't just about technical prowess; it's about the collective. He places a premium on player movement, believing that constant motion on the pitch makes a team more difficult to defend against. His teams press relentlessly, win the ball back quickly, and launch counter-attacks with precision.

"The challenge is to stay cool enough to handle the pressure in the moment so that you can succeed in the future," Klopp remarked. He understands that success is a process, a journey filled with challenges and setbacks. It's about staying focused on the long-term goal, even in the face of adversity.

## A Legacy Beyond Trophies

Klopp's arrival at Liverpool marked the beginning of a new era. He not only delivered trophies but instilled a winning mentality and a sense of unity within the club. The Premier League title and Champions League triumphs were symbols of his impact, but the Anfield faithful cherish him for much more.

"The more you do with the ball, the more you play with the ball, the better you get," he emphasised. His commitment to player development, both on and off the pitch, has been a defining feature of his managerial career. He knows that nurturing young talents is not just about winning today but building a legacy for the future.

Beyond the pitch, Klopp's involvement in charitable endeavours and community engagement initiatives showcases his dedication to making a positive impact on society. He knows the responsibility that comes with his platform and uses it to uplift others.

"I don't feel too much pressure. I only see an opportunity," he remarked. His approach to football is not burdened by the weight of expectations but fueled by the prospect of achieving something special. It's an attitude that has inspired his players and endeared him to fans.

His impact on football, his players, and the communities he touched will live on for generations. His journey is a testament to the power of passion, hard work, and authenticity. As one chapter closes, the football world eagerly awaits the next instalment of Jurgen Klopp's storied career. Whether on the sidelines or in a different role, his love for the game will continue to inspire and captivate, reminding us all why we fell in love with football in the first place.

# REFERENCES

- Roper, M. (2020, June 26). Jurgen Klopp's incredible rise from humble beginnings to Liverpool's Premier League title hero. Irish Mirror. Retrieved from https://www.irishmirror.ie/sport/soccer/soccer-news/jurgen-klopps-incredible-rise-humble-22260374
- Hunter, A. (2019, May 31). How a gut decision began Jürgen Klopp's managerial rollercoaster. The Guardian. Retrieved from https://www.theguardian.com/football/2019/may/31/jurgen-klopp-champions-league-final-liverpool-mainz
- Honigstein, R. (2017). *Bring The Noise: The Jürgen Klopp Story*. Penguin Books.
- Sports Illustrated. (2019, July 12). Jurgen Klopp: The Early Years at Mainz 05 Where He Sealed "Greatest Achievement." Retrieved August 4, 2023, from https://www.si.com/soccer/2019/07/12/jurgen-klopp-early-years-mainz-05-where-he-sealed-greatest-achievement
- Jürgen Klopp. (2023, August 4). In Wikipedia.

Retrieved from https://en.wikipedia.org/wiki/Jürgen_Klopp

- Jones, C. (2012, April 19). Jürgen Klopp's best quotes as Borussia Dortmund boss. Bleacher Report. Retrieved August 4, 2023, from https://bleacherreport.com/articles/2431383-jurgen-klopp-best-quotes-as-borussia-dortmund-boss

- Bundesliga.com. (2017, August 1). Yellow Wall: A wiki to Borussia Dortmund's Signal Iduna Park and BVB. Retrieved August 4, 2023, from https://www.bundesliga.com/en/news/Bundesliga/yellow-wall-wiki-borussia-dortmund-signal-iduna-park-bvb-474447.jsp

- Burt, J. (2013, May 21). Jürgen Klopp: Borussia Dortmund's 'normal one'. The Guardian. Retrieved August 4, 2023, from https://www.theguardian.com/football/2013/may/21/jurgen-klopp-borussia-dortmund-champions-league

- Bundesliga.com. (2015, July 1). Jürgen Klopp - Bundesliga legend. Retrieved August 4, 2023, from https://www.bundesliga.com/en/news/Bundesliga/0000317895.jsp

- Durkan, J. (2022, October 19) 5 of the best quotes from Jurgen Klopp's 1st Liverpool press conference. This is Anfield. Retrieved August 4, 2023, from https://www.thisisanfield.com/2022/10/5-of-the-best-quotes-from-jurgen-klopps-1st-liverpool-press-conference/

- Lusby, J. (2016, June 23). Jürgen Klopp explains Sadio Mané signing, says he's followed him for years. This is Anfield. Retrieved October 30, 2023, from https://www.thisisanfield.com/2016/06/ jurgen-klopp-explains-sadio-mane-signing-says-hes-followed-him-for-years/
- Cox, M. (2020, April 17). Why Jurgen Klopp's gegenpressing with Dortmund was revolutionary. Sky Sports. Retrieved October 29, 2023, from https://www.skysports.com/ football/news/11667/11925573/why-jurgen-klopps-gegenpressing-with-dortmund-was-revolutionary
- Liverpool FC. (2019, May 8). Jurgen Klopp reaction: Liverpool 4-0 Barcelona (4-3 agg): 'It's a special night, very special'. Liverpool FC. Retrieved October 29, 2023, from https:// www.liverpoolfc.com/news/first-team/349382-jurgen-klopp-reaction-liverpool-barcelona
- Liverpool FC. (2023, October 30). Jurgen Klopp Champions League final reaction: 'Tonight the boys showed it, goals in the right moment'. Liverpool FC. Retrieved October 30, 2023, from https://www.liverpoolfc.com/ news/first-team/351532-jurgen-klopp-champions-league-final-reaction
- McNulty, P. (2020, June 25). Liverpool: Jurgen Klopp's best quotes after Premier League title win. The Independent. Retrieved October 30,

2023, from https://www.independent.co.uk/sport/football/premier-league/liverpool-jurgen-klopp-best-quotes-premier-league-title-win-a9586646.html

- Planet Football. (2022, February 1). 13 quotes to explain Jurgen Klopp's philosophy: "I always want it loud - win or lose". Planet Football. Retrieved October 30, 2023, from https://www.planetfootball.com/quick-reads/13-quotes-to-explain-jurgen-klopps-philosophy-i-always-want-it-loud
- Liverpool FC. (2019, May 25). Jurgen Klopp: Leadership interview. Liverpool FC. Retrieved October 30, 2023, from https://www.liverpoolfc.com/news/first-team/351529-jurgen-klopp-leadership-interview-liverpool
- Pearce, J. (2022, April 28). Jurgen Klopp reveals his wife's role in extending Liverpool stay. This Is Anfield. Retrieved October 30, 2023, from https://www.thisisanfield.com/2022/04/jurgen-klopp-reveals-his-wifes-role-in-extending-liverpool-stay/
- Jones, N. (2018, August 1). Klopp reveals what he really thinks about the media - and why he regrets Neville brothers spat. Goal.com. Retrieved October 30, 2023, from https://www.goal.com/en/news/klopp-reveals-what-he-really-thinks-about-the-media---and-why-he-regrets-neville-brothers-

spat/1a94lu8q8ykrd1wbiq4iz0khqt
- Oiley, J. (2022, May 13). Liverpool: Jurgen Klopp 'master of being underdog' - Chelsea boss Thomas Tuchel. ESPN. Retrieved October 30, 2023, from https://www.espn.com/soccer/story/_/id/37628413/liverpool-jurgen-klopp-master-being-underdog-chelsea-boss-thomas-tuchel
- Jones, G. (2019, September 24). Jurgen Klopp joins charity movement. The Fan Network. Retrieved November 1, 2023, from https://tfn.scot/news/jurgen-klopp-joins-charity-movement
- Addison, M. (2023, July 23). Liverpool Anfield expansion: Incredible view from seats emerges as Jürgen Klopp 'can't wait'. Liverpool.com. Retrieved November 1, 2023, from https://www.liverpool.com/liverpool-fc-news/features/liverpool-anfield-expansion-seats-klopp-27378339
- TopTekkers. (2020, March 9). Jurgen Klopp on player development. TopTekkers. Retrieved November 1, 2023, from https://www.toptekkers.com/blog/jurgen-klopp-on-player-development-toptekkers
- Goal. (2020, September 16). Klopp confirms his plans for life after Liverpool & promises he won't manage new club straight away. Goal. Retrieved November 1, 2023, from https://www.goal.com/en/news/klopp-confirms-his-plans-for-life-after-liverpool--promises-he-

wont-manage-new-club-straight-away/3hjyf2bcnnaj1l4d6romxbaqo
- Marsh, D. (2023, September 10). Jurgen Klopp Liverpool Germany Flick. Mirror. Retrieved November 1, 2023, from https://www.mirror.co.uk/sport/football/news/jurgen-klopp-liverpool-germany-flick-30906377
- BrainyQuote. (n.d.). Jurgen Klopp Quotes. Retrieved November 1, 2023, from https://www.brainyquote.com/authors/jurgen-klopp-quotes
- The Guardian. (2013, May 26). Champions League final quotes. Retrieved November 1, 2023, from https://www.theguardian.com/football/2013/may/25/champions-league-final-quotes
- Dutton, J. (2018, May 22). Jurgen Klopp reveals how he masterminded victory over Real Madrid with Borussia Dortmund... and aims to repeat the trick with Liverpool. MailOnline. Retrieved November 4, 2023, from https://www.dailymail.co.uk/sport/football/article-5759729/Jurgen-Klopp-masterminded-victory-Real-Madrid-Borussia-Dortmund.html
- PA Sport. (2019, May 12). Klopp congratulates champions Man City after losing out to them in title race. Eurosport. Retrieved November 4, 2023, from https://www.eurosport.com/football/klopp-congratulates-champions-

man-city-after-losing-out-to-them-in-title-race_sto7268301/story.shtml

- Gott, T. (2022, September 8) Jurgen Klopp's final year at Borussia Dortmund: What happened? 90min.com. Retrieved November 4, 2023, from https://www.90min.com/posts/jurgen-klopp-final-year-borussia-dortmund-what-happened

- Joshi, V. (2020, April 27). *Top of the Klopps: 10 funniest quotes from Jurgen Klopp over the years.* Sportskeeda. Retrieved August 4, 2023, from https://www.sportskeeda.com/football/top-of-the-klopps-10-funniest-quotes-from-jurgen-klopp-over-the-years

- Cooke, R. (2018, July 19). Jurgen Klopp defends Liverpool spending following Alisson signing. Sky Sports. Retrieved November 4, 2023, from https://www.skysports.com/football/news/11669/11445018/jurgen-klopp-defends-liverpool-spending-following-alisson-signing

- Liverpool Football Club. (2023, November 4). *Jürgen Klopp's verdict on Liverpool's Champions League final win.* Retrieved November 4, 2023, from https://www.liverpoolfc.com/news/first-team/303029-jurgen-klopp-reaction-liverpool-fc-champions-league-final

- Carroll, J., Shaw, C., & Williams, S. (2022, May 28). Jürgen Klopp's verdict on Champions League final defeat.

Liverpool FC. Retrieved August 4, 2023, from https://www.liverpoolfc.com/news/ jurgen-klopps-verdict-on-champions-league- final-defeat

- Evangelical Focus. (2019, January 11). Jürgen Klopp: "Jesus is the most important person in history". Retrieved August 4, 2023, from https://evangelicalfocus.com/life- tech/4134/jurgen-klopp-jesus-is-the-most- important-person-in-history

- Hunter, S. (2015, October 29). Ibe: Klopp is like a father figure. Liverpool Football Club. Retrieved November 4, 2023, from https:// www.liverpoolfc.com/news/first- team/200956-ibe-klopp-is-like-a-father- figure

- Rice-Coates, C. (2019, August 15). Liverpool: Jurgen Klopp on Wolfgang Frank, the perfect role model who influenced him more than any other. Liverpool Echo. Retrieved November 4, 2023, from https://www.liverpoolecho.co.uk/ sport/football/football-news/liverpool- jurgen-klopp-wolfgang-frank-16745261

- Carroll, J. (2016, May 18). Jürgen Klopp on Liverpool's Europa League final defeat. Liverpool FC. Retrieved August 4, 2023, from https://www.liverpoolfc.com/news/first- team/222489-jurgen-klopp-on-liverpool-s- europa-league-final-defeat

- Planet Football. (2019, November 20). 13 players who say Jurgen

Klopp improved them: Mané, Reus, Van Dijk. https://www.planetfootball.com/quick-reads/13-players-who-say-jurgen-klopp-improved-them-mane-reus-van-dijk

- Wells, D. (2019, September 6). Jurgen Klopp reveals hilarious antics after Borussia Dortmund's 2011 title-winning celebrations. Mirror Online. Retrieved September 6, 2023, from https://www.mirror.co.uk/sport/football/news/jurgen-klopp-reveals-hilarious-antics-19574092

- Addison, M. (2019, August 14). The whole changing room was on the floor laughing - Wijnaldum tells hilarious Klopp story from 2018 CL final. Empire of the Kop. Retrieved September 6, 2023, from https://www.empireofthekop.com/2019/08/14/the-whole-changing-room-was-on-the-floor-laughing-wijnaldum-tells-hilarious-klopp-story-from-2018-cl-final/

- Klopp, J. (2019, September 24). Maybe I am dreaming. The Players' Tribune. Retrieved November 6, 2023, from https://www.theplayerstribune.com/articles/jurgen-klopp-liverpool-fc

- Irish Mirror. (2019, May 20). Mario Gotze tells hilarious story about Jurgen Klopp's hair transplant. Irish Mirror. Retrieved November 6, 2023, from https://www.irishmirror.ie/sport/soccer/soccer-news/mario-gotze-tells-hilarious-story-16172739

- Price, G, Shaw, C.(October 8, 2015). Timeline and inside story of Jürgen Klopp's arrival at Liverpool. Liverpool FC. Retrieved November 6, 2023, from https://www.liverpoolfc.com/news/timeline-and-inside-story-jurgen-klopps-arrival-liverpool
- Herbert, I. (2016, November 18). It was Santa Claus: Klopp tells hilarious story of Bundesliga Christmas party as he leaps to Wayne Rooney's defence. Independent.ie. Retrieved November 6, 2023, from https://www.independent.ie/sport/soccer/premier-league/it-was-santa-claus-klopp-tells-hilarious-story-of-bundesliga-christmas-party-as-he-leaps-to-wayne-rooneys-defence/35225290.html
- Stead, M. (2018, October 12). *Klopp explains that celebration after West Brom draw.* Football365. Retrieved November 6, 2023, from https://www.football365.com/news/klopp-explains-that-celebration-after-west-brom-draw
- Sheringham, S. (2020, March 23). Jurgen Klopp: Liverpool manager's journey from Black Forest to heroic status at Anfield. BBC Sport. Retrieved November 6, 2023, from https://www.bbc.com/sport/football/51989229
- Ladson, M. (2019, December 22). What does Liverpool's Club World Cup victory mean for the rest of their season? FourFourTwo. Retrieved November

6, 2023, from https://www.fourfourtwo.com/ features/liverpools-club-world-cup-victory-win-premier-league-season-matt-ladson

- Linning, S. Jurgen Klopp's secret weapon. Daily Mail. Retrieved November 6, 2023, from https://www.dailymail.co.uk/femail/ article-10856211/Liverpool-manager-Jurgen-Klopps-wife-secret-weapon.html

- Victor, T. (2016, September 26). Watch: Jurgen Klopp explains how being a TV pundit changed his career. SportsJOE.ie. Retrieved November 8, 2023, from https:// www.sportsjoe.ie/football/sky-sports-welcome-jurgen-klopp-mnf-96780

- Deutsche Welle (DW). (2016, September 27). Jürgen Klopp charms British audience. Retrieved November 8, 2023, from https:// www.dw.com/en/brits-fall-for-klopps-charm-as-he-turns-tv-pundit/ a-35899369#:~:text=Liverpool's%20manager %20was%20Sky's%20guest,is%20soaring %20in%20the%20UK

- Planet Football. (2023, June 16). 13 quotes to explain Jurgen Klopp's philosophy: 'I always want it loud'. Retrieved November 8, 2023, from https://www.planetfootball.com/quick-reads/13-quotes-to-explain-jurgen-klopps-philosophy-i-always-want-it-loud

- Shaw, C. (2021, September 23). 'Great news, very exciting' - Jürgen Klopp hails Anfield Road expansion. Liverpool FC. Retrieved

November 9, 2023, from https://www.liverpoolfc.com/news/first-team/444459-great-news-very-exciting-jurgen-klopp-hails-anfield-road-expansion

- MacDonald, K. (2022, July 1). What's next for Anfield expansion after stunning new footage released. Liverpool Echo. Retrieved November 9, 2023, from https://www.liverpoolecho.co.uk/sport/football/football-news/whats-next-anfield-expansion-after-24371695
- Neveling, E. (2016). Jürgen Klopp: The Biography. Ebury Press.
- Liverpool FC. (2018, December 2). Jürgen Klopp's reaction: Liverpool 1-0 Everton. Liverpool FC. Retrieved from https://www.liverpoolfc.com/news/first-team/328054-jurgen-klopp-reaction-liverpool-everton
- Lusby, J. (2018, May 2). Video: Jurgen Klopp post-match press conference – Roma 4-2 Liverpool (6-7 agg). This Is Anfield. https://www.thisisanfield.com/2018/05/video-jurgen-klopp-post-match-press-conference-roma-4-2-liverpool-6-7-agg/
- Carroll, J. (2020, June 25). Jürgen Klopp exclusive: 'My message is: Winning the Premier League is for you.' Liverpool FC. https://www.liverpoolfc.com/news/first-team/404360-jurgen-klopp-exclusive-my-message-is-winning-the-premier-league-is-

for-you

Printed in Great Britain
by Amazon